CONTENTS

INTRODUCTION 10

WHAT TO EAT AND AVOID ON THE KETO DIET 11

Meat and poultry 11

Dairy 12

Eggs 12

Fish and Seafood 13

Nuts and Seeds 13

Oils and fats 14

Vegetables 14

Fruits 15

Berries 15

Beans and legumes 15

Condiments 16

Grain products 16

Beverages 17

Sweets 18

Others 18

TOP 10 INSTANT POT TIPS 19

TOP 10 KETO DIET TIPS 21

BREAKFAST 25

Breakfast Casserole 25

Eggs Benedict 25

Starbucks Eggs 25

Frittata with Greens 26

Egg Cups 26

Bacon and Cheese Bites 27

Noatmeal 27

Breakfast Sandwich 28

Morning Burritos 28

White Cabbage Hash Browns 28

Giant Vanilla Pancake 29

Meat Cups 29

Bell Peppers with Omelet 30

Bacon Avocado Bomb 30

Stuffed Hard-Boiled Eggs 30
Cheese Roll-Ups 31
Breakfast Taco Skillet 31
Meat and Cauliflower Bake 32
Pulled Pork Hash with Eggs 32
Kale and Eggs Bake 32
Bacon Casserole 33
Swedish Meatballs 33
Egg Cups on the Run 34
Margherita Egg Cups 34

APPETIZERS AND SIDES **35**
Cauliflower Queso 35
Sweet Smokies 35
Rosemary Chicken Wings 35
Classic Meatballs 36
Bacon Deviled Eggs 36
Spinach Dip 37
Sausage Balls 37
BLT Dip 37
Taco Bites 38
Sausage Dip 38
Stuffed Mushrooms 38
Cheese Jalapenos 39
Coconut Shrimps 39
Scallion Dip 40
Eggplant Bites 40
Bacon Peppers 40
Fat Bombs..41
Chicken Celery Sticks 41
Reuben Pickles 41
Parmesan Balls with Greens 42
Cheese Stuffed Shishito Peppers 42
Roasted Tomatillos 43
Chicken&Chinese Cabbage Salad 43
Cauliflower Fritters 43
Zucchini Cheese Tots 44
Red Cauliflower Rice 44
Steamed Spinach with Garlic..44

Lemon Mushrooms 45
Feta Psiti 45
Steamed Savoy Cabbage 45
Sesame Broccoli Sprouts 46
Faux-Tatoes 46
Steamed Kohlrabi 46
Broccoli Skewers 47
Garlic Shirataki Noodles 47
Steamed Fennel Bulb 47
Shrimp Sandwich 48

SOUP AND STEWS **49**
Broccoli Cheese Soup 49
Gumbo 49
Chicken Soup 49
Taco Soup 50
Tuscan Soup 50
Cheeseburger Soup 51
Cabbage Soup 51
Cauliflower Soup 51
Beef Stew 52
Curry Stew with Chicken 52
Chicken Paprikash 52
Pork Stew 53
Italian Style Lamb Stew 53
Cheesy Cream Soup 54
Seafood Stew 54
Okra and Beef Stew 54
Chipotle Stew 55
Keto Chili 55
Pizza Soup 55
Lamb Soup 56
Minestrone Soup 56
Chorizo Soup 57
Red Feta Soup 57
"Ramen" Soup 57
Beef Tagine 58

BEEF AND LAMB **59**
Beef Pot Roast 59

Mongolian Beef 59
Thyme Beef Brisket 59
Goulash 60
Beef Pot Round Steak 60
Steak Bites 60
Hibachi Steak 61
Beef Burgundy 61
Beef Gyros Stuffing 62
Butter Beef 62
Lamb Shank with Spices 62
Greek Style Leg of Lamb 62
Lamb Curry 63
Persian Lamb 63
Lamb Roast 64
Lamb Kleftiko 64
Lamb Bhuna 64
Beef Vindaloo 65
Lamb Masala 65
Rogan Josh 65
Icelandic Lamb 66
Harissa Lamb Shoulder 66
Kofta Curry 67
Pesto Rack of Lamb 67
Koobideh 67
Shami Kabob 68
Lamb Burger 68
Steamed Rostelle 69
Veal Meatloaf 69
Peppered Lamb Ribs 70

PORK **71**
Pork Chops with Blue Cheese 71
Carnitas Pulled Pork 71
Sweet Pork Tenderloin 71
Thyme Pork Meatballs 72
Asian Ribs 72
Mississippi Pork 73
BBQ Baby Back Ribs 73
Vietnamese Pork 73

Pork Tenders 74

Stuffed Pork Rolls 74

Aromatic Pork Belly 74

Ranch Pork Chops 75

Paprika Ribs 75

Wrapped Pork Cubes 75

Herbed Pork Tenderloin 76

Cilantro Pork Shoulder 76

Peppercorn Pork 76

Pork Ragu 77

Apple Cider Vinegar Ham 77

Smothered Pork Chops 78

Meatloaf with Eggs 78

Turmeric Pork Strips 78

Fabulous Cilantro Meatballs 79

Basil Pork Loin 79

Ground Pork Stroganoff 80

Stew Cubes 80

Pork Milanese 80

Romano Pork Chops 81

Ground Pork Pizza Crust 81

Pork Chops Al Pastor 82

Taco Casserole 82

Mozzarella Stuffed Meatballs 82

Smoked Sausages Cabbage 83

Sub Salad 83

POULTRY 84

Garlic Chicken with Lemon 84

Tuscan Chicken 84

Crack Chicken 84

White Chicken Chili 85

Juicy Chicken Breast 85

Chicken in Gravy 86

Mustard Chicken Breast 86

Butter Chicken 86

Parmesan Chicken Fillets 87

Chicken Alfredo 87

Paprika Chicken Wings 88

Cordon Bleu 88
Herbed Whole Chicken 88
Chicken Pasta 89
Fiesta Chicken 89
Pulled Chicken 90
Chicken Masala 90
Sesame Chicken 90
Chicken Curry with Cilantro 91
Tender Chicken Thighs 91
Chicken Jalapenos Roll 91
Chicken Nuggets 92
Fajita Strips 92
Thyme Chicken Gizzards 93
Greek Burger 93
Dijon Turkey Meatballs 93
Tender Turkey Tetrazzini 94
Smoky Chicken Breast 94
Cheese Chicken Kofte 94
Poblano Chicken Strips 95
Chicken Lombardy 95
Chicken with Pizza Stuffing 96
Philadelphia Stuffed Chicken Breast 96
Chicken Fingers 96
Pancetta Wings 97
Provolone Stuffed Chicken 97

FISH AND SEAFOOD **98**
Cioppino Stew 98
Bang Bang Shrimps 98
Apple Cider Vinegar Mussels 98
Thyme Lobster Tails 99
Blackened Salmon 99
Shrimp Curry with Coconut Milk 99
Alaskan Crab Legs 100
Cajun Cod 100
Louisiana Gumbo 100
Lemon Salmon 101
Boiled Crawfish 101
Spinach Tuna Cakes 101

Spicy Cod 102

Pulpo Gallego 102

Chili Haddock 103

Clam Chowder 103

Italian Style Salmon 103

Butter Clams..104

Fish Curry 104

Shrimp Skewers 104

Salmon Cakes 105

Rosemary Catfish Steak 105

Lime Mahi Mahi 105

Pesto Flounder 106

Salmon Caprese 106

Seafood Zoodle Alfredo 107

Cod with Olives 107

VEGAN **108**

Cauliflower Tikka Masala 108

Spiced Cauliflower Head 108

Parm Zucchini Noodles 108

Tempeh Satay 109

Teriyaki Eggplants 109

Kale Stir Fry..109

Tofu Quiche 110

Thyme Cabbage...110

Herbed Radish 111

Jicama Mash 111

Spiced Broccoli 111

Cauliflower Gnocchi 112

Chives Mushrooms 112

Zucchini Fritters 112

Mashed Turnips...113

DESSERTS..**114**

Pumpkin Pie Spices Cheesecake 114

Daikon Cake 114

Almond Pie..115

Coconut Cupcakes 115

Anise Hot Chocolate 115

Chocolate Mousse 116

Lime Muffins...116

Blueberry Muffins..117

Low Carb Brownie 117

Pecan Pie 118

Vanilla Flan...118

Vanilla Pie..119

Custard 119

Crème Brule...119

Lava Cake 120

Cinnamon Roll 120

Peanut Bars...121

Cocoa Cookie 121

Red Velvet Muffins...121

Pecan Pralines...122

Vanilla Hot Drink 122

RECIPE INDEX... **123**

INTRODUCTION

My story has started a long time before I decided to be slim. Ever since childhood, I was overweight. During the teen time, my situation wasn't so deplorable. I am grateful to my family because they always accepted me as I am. But it wasn't enough for me because all around hated me. At the age of 15, I understood that I am unshapely girl. I was in graduation class, my weight has already exceeded 270 lbs. I felt like I am a giant cow who couldn't fit into any sexy dress for a prom party. My parents have never been worried about weight, they just repeated all the time "you are an angel, you are beautiful". I knew that it wasn't true, in the mirror I saw plum girl. After graduating from school, I became very depressed. All my troubles I jammed with tones of chocolate and Coke.

One sunny day I firmly decided for myself - enough for me! I don't want to live like that anymore. I will be changed. I had made the "wish map", where I was slim and smiling, and started to do sports and eat fewer sweets and sparkling drinks. I couldn't say that it wasn't successful but I didn't get the desired result. I wanted everything at once, so I even practiced fasting. I could drink water and vegetable smoothies for 2-3 days. But it all ended with me breaking down and gaining even more weight. At that time, I already started having health problems. I could not walk for a long time, I was haunted by headaches, pain in my stomach, as well as bad breath.

I decided to go to the doctor and do a comprehensive analysis of the whole body. When my doctor looked at my tests, he advised going to a nutritionist. This time I discovered a ketogenic diet. The doctor didn't prescribe something special. It was a certain diet and simple physical exercises every day. But I have to eat a lot of proteins, and almost no vegetables (I hated them at that time). I couldn't believe that everything is so easy! But I didn't lose faith and clearly followed the doctor's instructions. After a week of keto life, I did not see significant results, but after 2 weeks the arrows of the scales showed -8 lbs. During the year of keto lifestyle, my weight dropped by 83 lbs and my health became better. I cried with happiness! Finally, I did it! This is just a miracle! Now I am a wife, mom, and just happy woman!

I wrote this book to help people like me. To those who still think that they are hopeless! I am sure that this diet will change your way of thinking and make a big difference in your life. I am the greatest example that nothing is impossible. You should know that losing weight is not only restrictions and starving. The real-life on keto diet exists and this book proves it! Our mind and our body are omnipotent! They know well what we need! Each of us should be dropkicked to take the path of a happy life! I strongly believe that this book will be a guide and silver lining in a better version of you!

WHAT TO EAT AND AVOID ON THE KETO DIET

Meat and poultry

Actually, it is the primary type of food for the Keto diet. It contains 0% of carbs and is rich in potassium, selenium, zinc, and B vitamins. Grass-fed meat and poultry are the most beneficial. It caused by high omega 3 fats and antioxidants content. Bear in mind that Keto diet is a high-fat diet and high consumption of proteins can cause to harder getting of ketosis.

What to eat	Enjoy occasionally	What to avoid
• chicken	• bacon	• breaded meats
• duck	• ham	• processed meats
• goose	• low-fat meat, such as skinless chicken breast	
• ground beef	• sausage	
• lamb		
• ostrich		
• partridge		
• pheasant		
• pork		
• quail		
• turkey		
• venison		

Dairy

High-fat dairy products are awesome for the keto diet. They are calcium-rich full-fat dairy product is nutritious and can make you full longer. Milk lovers should restrict or even cross out this product from the daily meal plan. It is allowed only 1 tablespoon of milk in your drink per day but doesn't abuse it daily.

What to eat	What to avoid
• butter	• fat-free yogurt
• cheese (soft and hard)	• low-fat cheese
• full-fat yogurt	• milk
• heavy cream	• skim milk
• sour cream	• skim mozzarella
	• sweetened yogurt

Eggs

This is the most wholesome food in the world. Use them everywhere you want! Containing less than one gram of carbohydrates, eggs are a wonderful food for the keto lifestyle. Eating eggs reducing the risk of heart disease and save your eyes health.

Note: free-range eggs are healthier options for the keto diet.

What to avoid	
• chicken eggs	• ostrich eggs
• duck eggs	• quail eggs
• goose eggs	

Fish and Seafood

Fatty fish as salmon is beneficial for the keto diet. Small fish like sardines, herring, etc. are less in toxins. The best option for a keto diet is wild-caught seafood; it has a higher number of omega 3 fats. Scientifically proved that frequent eating of fish improves mental health.

What to eat		What to avoid
• catfish	• prawns	• breaded fish
• clams	• salmon	
• cod	• sardines	
• crab	• scallops	
• halibut	• shrimp	
• herring	• snapper	
• lobster	• swordfish	
• mackerel	• tilapia	
• Mahi Mahi	• trout	
• mussels	• tuna	
• oysters		

Nuts and Seeds

These products are heart-healthy and fiber-rich. Nevertheless, eat nuts and seeds as a snack is a bad idea. As usual, the amount of eaten food can be much more than allowed. Nuts like cashews are very insidious and contain a lot of carbohydrates. Replace them with macadamia or pecan.

What to eat		What to avoid
• almonds	• peanuts	• cashews
• chia seeds	• pecans	• pistachio
• flaxseeds	• pumpkin seeds	• chocolate-covered nuts
• hazelnuts	• walnuts	• nut butter (sweetened)
• nut butter (unsweetened)	• macadamia nuts	

Oils and fats

It is the main component of the keto-friendly sauces and dressings.

Olive oil and coconut oil are highly recommending for everyone who decided to follow the keto diet. They are almost perfect it their fatty acid composition. Avoid artificial trans fats which are poison for our body. This type of fats, as usual, used in French fries, margarine, and crackers.

What to eat	What to avoid
• avocado oil	• grapeseed oil
• coconut oil	• canola oil
• hazelnut oil	• cottonseed oil
• olive oil	• hydrogenated oils
• pumpkin seed oil	• margarine
• sesame oil	• peanut oil
• walnut oil	• soybean oil
	• safflower oil
	• processed vegetable oils

Vegetables

Keto diet cannot work without vegetables, but their usage should be in moderation. Starchy vegetables such as potatoes, sweet potatoes, etc. are deadly for our body and will not bring anything more than overweight. At the same time, vegetables that are low in carbs, are rich in antioxidants and can protect the body from free radicals that damage our cells.

What to eat		What to avoid
• asparagus	• mushrooms	• carrots
• avocado	• olives	• corn
• broccoli	• onions	• beets
• cabbage	• tomatoes	• butternut squash
• cauliflower	• peppers	• parsnips
• celery	• spinach	• potatoes (both sweet and regular)
• cucumber	• zucchini	
• eggplant	• other nonstarchy vegetables	• pumpkin
• leafy greens		• turnips
• lettuce		• yams
		• yuca
		• other starchy vegetables

Fruits

This type of food is high in carbs that's why they should be limited while keto diet. Besides this, almost all fruits are high in glucose and can enhance blood sugar.

Enjoy occasionally	What to avoid	
• lemons	• apples	• peaches
• pomegranates	• bananas	• pears
• limes	• grapefruits	• pineapple
	• limes	• plums
	• mango	• dried fruits
	• oranges	

Berries

If you are looking for how to substitute fruits, this is your godsend. Berries contain up to 12 grams of net carbs per 3.5 ounces serving. They are high in fiber and can maintain the health of your body and fight with diseases. Note consumption of a huge amount of berries can be harmful.

Enjoy occasionally	What to avoid
• blackberries	• cherries
• blueberries	• grapes
• raspberries	• melon
• strawberries	• watermelon

Beans and legumes

There are no ingredients in this food group that would be healthy for a keto diet. Beans and legumes contain fewer carbs in comparison with root vegetables such as potatoes; nevertheless, this type of carbohydrates fastly adds up.

What to avoid	
• black beans	• navy beans
• chickpeas	• peas
• kidney beans	• pinto beans
• lentils	• soybeans

Condiments

Condiments can make any type of meal awesome. Even a piece of meat will turn into the masterpiece with them. There are only a few products which are better to avoid; nevertheless, nowadays, you can find keto-friendly substitutors in a supermarket.

One more hot tip: putting hot pepper in your meal will reduce the amount of salt you need and make the taste of the dish more saturated.

What to eat	What to avoid
• herbs and spices	• BBQ sauce
• lemon juice	• hot sauces
• mayonnaise with no added sugar	• ketchup
• salad dressings with no added sugar	• maple syrup
• salt and pepper	• salad dressings with added sugar
• vinegar	• sweet dipping sauces
	• tomato sauce

Grain products

Actually, it is needless to say that all grains are forbidden and can't be eaten if you want to achieve ketosis. Grains contain complex carbohydrates that have a feature to be absorbed slower than simple carbohydrates. For better understanding, if the food has keto-friendly carbs, look at the number of starch and sugar. Their number should be minimum.

What to avoid	
• baked goods	• muesli
• bread	• oats
• cereal	• pasta
• corn	• pizza
• crackers	• popcorn
• flour	• rice
• granola	• wheat

Beverages

A variety of keto drinks may shock you. Probably you know that the best beverage for a keto diet is water. Nevertheless, in order to brighten up a little gray everyday life of keto lovers, the consumption of alcoholic beverages is allowed in moderation. For instance, pure forms of alcohol, such as gin, vodka, or tequila can be drunk once per week. They contain zero amounts of carbs. Avoid all sweetened beverages; they are a priori high carbohydrate.

What to eat	Enjoy occasionally	What to avoid
• almond milk	• dry wine	• alcoholic drinks (sweetened)
• bone broth	• hard liquor	• beer
• coffee (unsweetened)	• vodka	• cider
• flax milk	• other low carb alcoholic drinks	• coffee (sweetened)
• tea (unsweetened)		• fruit juice
• water (still and sparkling)		• soda
		• sports drinks
		• smoothies
		• tea (sweetened)
		• wines (sweet)

Sweets

Cakes and cookies cannot help in losing weight in any diet. As for keto, here everything is strict with this. You should try to avoid sugar and sweeteners in any form. Moreover, sweets negatively affect blood sugar and insulin levels.

Enjoy occasionally	What to avoid	
• erythritol	• artificial sweeteners	• ice cream
• stevia	• buns	• pastries
• sucralose	• candy	• pies
	• cakes	• pudding
	• chocolate	• sugar
	• cookies	• tarts
	• custard	

Others

Fast food and processed food contain a huge amount of stabilizers and harmful carbohydrates. The main rule of the Keto diet is avoiding sugar. 99,9% of such food contains harmful sugars. The existence of which in the body negates the achievement of ketosis.

What to avoid
• fast food
• processed foods

TOP 10 INSTANT POT TIPS

1.   Flavored liquids enhance your meal.

Broths, juices, dairies, and stocks can enhance the taste of your meal. This kind of liquids has the property not only to convey its taste but also the taste of spices that were used while cooking. Don't be afraid of experiments! The mixture of chicken beef broth and sautéed garlic instead of ordinary water will turn the lean rice on a flavored meal.

2.   Cook by small pieces instead of the whole product.

You can reduce the cooking time almost two times by chopping the ingredients into small pieces. Doing this, the pressure and steam will reach the ingredients evenly and will cook them faster.

3.   Make the sauces and gravies after cooking.

Thickening liquids is a good way to get delicious gravies; they can improve the taste of your dish. The best liquid thickeners are starch and flour. Adding them in the last minutes of cooking will make the texture of the meal more saturated and uniform. Also, this method helps not to overcook the ingredients, do not deprive them of vitamins and as a result, make the food healthier.

4.   A steaming rack is a good option for any meal.

Almost all Instant pot models come with steamer rack that is essential not only for cooking vegetables. This tool can be appropriate at any time when you want to cook the ingredients with less amount of liquids. Such food as pies, fish, or meat will have a completely different taste if you use steamer rack while cooking.

5.   Use improvised things.

Nowadays, the market suggests a huge variety of accessories for instant pot. Some of them have important meaning but some can be substitute by simple things. For instance, foil can be a wonderful replacement for instant pot trays and molds. It can take any form and has non-stick features. Use it for cooking muffins, pies, and even meatloaves.

6.   Cooking with pressure can take more time.

As a rule, it takes approximately 10-15 minutes to reach the needed pressure in the inner pot. Very rarely the recipes include this time in the total cooking time; that's to accurately determine the cooking time and notify your family when it is time to eat, add extra minutes to the cooking time specified in the recipe.

7. Cook two or more meals per one time.

The instant pot comes with only one inner pot, which is not always convenient when cooking several dishes. Therefore, nimble housewives found an excellent life hack on how to save time not only on cooking but also on washing dishes. To do this, simply purchase a few more inner pots and cook meals more quickly.

8. Get rid of odors.

Using the sealing rings will help you to avoid the odors. As usual, the smell of spices after cooking meat, fish, or vegetable meals are very strong. That's why it is highly recommended to buy extra sealing rings for all the most popular types of meal you cook; so each dish can retain its unique taste and flavor.

9. Easy cleaning.

Use a dishwasher to wash all removable parts of the instant pot. Detergent and a strong flow of water in the dishwasher will make your instant pot clean and at the same time save your time. For non-removable instant pot parts, use vinegar and lemon juice. They can make your kitchen appliance sparkle like new.

10. Clean nooks, so instant pot is always like new.

Sometimes the nooks of instant pot become clogged with sauces, steam after using pressure cooking mode or food leftovers that were accidentally spilled. Clean the nooks with the help of the brush and paper after each usage of the instant pot to preserve its original appearance for many years.

TOP 10 KETO DIET TIPS

1. Combine together Keto and Intermittent fasting.

Intermittent fasting (IF) is the right way to get ketosis. It gives your body additional benefits. Scientists showed that connection keto diet and intermittent fasting can up the results which can give only strict following of the keto diet.

IF means not eating and drinking during a determined amount of time. It is recommended to separate your day into a building phase (BP) and cleansing phase(CP); where the building phase is the time between the first and last time of eating (first-last); and cleansing is the opposite time (last-first). Start from 14-hours CP and 11-hours BP. Continue like this till your body adapts to the new daily plan. It can take 2-3 days. The first days will be the hardest but then you will feel relief and you can safely proceed to the next stage where BP turns into 5 hours and CP - into 19 hours.

According to research, women get the highest benefits of IF. It is possible to get rid of adrenal fatigue, hypothyroid, and hormonal imbalance.

2. Staying hydrated is essential.

Our body is 60% water. Water ensures the normal digestion of food and the absorption of nutrients from the intestines. If there is not enough water in the body, there will be discomfort in the abdomen and constipation. Drinking water is important even if you are not on keto.

The kidneys filter 5,000 ounces of blood per day so that the result is 50 ounces of urine. For the normal elimination of toxins and waste substances, you need to drink at least 50 ounces of water per day, but preferably more.

Many people face the problem of unwillingness to drink water. The best way to prevent dehydration and all its unpleasant consequences is to put a bottle or cup of water on the table and take a sip every time you look at the water. If you realize that you are thirsty, then eliminate thirst in time.

Regular drinking of the right amount of water for 1 week will become a habit and you will not be able to live differently.

3. Salt isn't harmful.

Salt plays an important role in complex metabolic processes. It is part of the blood, lymph, saliva, tears, gastric juice, bile - that is, all the fluids of our body. Any fluctuations in the salt content in the blood plasma lead to serious metabolic disorders

When fewer carbohydrates enter the body, insulin levels drop. Less insulin circulating in the body leads to secrete excess water in the kidneys instead of holding it. It means that salt and other important minerals and electrolytes are washed out of the body.

Replenish salt is possible by eating bone broths, cucumbers, celeriac, salty keto nuts, and seeds.

The best salts for keto diet are 2 types of salt. Pink salt has a more saturated, saltier taste, and contains calcium, magnesium, and potassium. Sea salt is simply evaporated seawater. The crystals of sea salt are slightly larger than iodized salt, and it has a stronger aroma. It contains potassium, magnesium, sulfur, phosphorus, and zinc.

4. Sport is important.

It is proved that physical activity improves the health of the whole body in general and accelerates metabolism. When we do sport, the first thing is we get rid of carbohydrates, and only then we burn fats. On a keto diet, even minimal physical activity contributes to the rapid decomposition of fats. You simply don't have glucose (carbohydrates) and any load breaks down fats. The most effective workouts on an empty stomach. Sports during keto are very comfortable. You do not feel hungry and can play sports without breakdowns and overeating. Your stamina is significantly increased. If the protein is correctly calculated, you don't lose muscle mass with a calorie deficit.

The combination of three types of workouts gives the best result for health, weight dynamics, and even mood! These are workouts, aerobic, and stretching. Start with small loads every day and increase it as you can. Do not forget to take measurements of your body to monitor the result!

5. Reduce stress.

Sometimes, observing all the postulates of the keto lifestyle, ketosis does not occur or occurs very slowly. In 99 cases, it happens due to the level of stress in your life. Thus, the hormone cortisol rises, the sympathetic nervous system is stimulated.

Cortisol is produced in response to any stress, even the most minor. How does it happen?

Cortisol "eats" our muscles to turn them into glucose, it catabolizes bones, which is fraught with osteoporosis, causes increased appetite, and suppresses immunity. It also causes increased production of glucose and insulin, and exactly this stops ketosis.

During keto-adaptation (the first 3 weeks), increased cortisol is produced, because the usual energy, glucose, ceases to flow into the body, and it turns on the "self-preservation mode".

It is very important at first to minimize stress from the outside, then everything will normalize.

You should be able to switch from stimulation of the sympathetic nervous system to parasympathetic. Stimulation of the parasympathetic nervous system contributes to the restoration and accumulation of energy resources. This can be achieved by a simple 15 minutes' meditation. The time when you cannot be interrupted.

6. Sleep above all!

Sleep and stress are two interconnected components. Lack of sleep leads to increased stress. Consequently, stress hormone levels and blood sugar levels rise and we gain weight very fast.

Doctors recommend an 8-9 hour sleep every day. The best time to fall asleep is before 11 pm. An hour before bedtime, try not to use any gadgets. It is better to spend this time in silence, meditation, listening to calm music or reading a paper book. Thus, we calm the nervous system and set it to sleep. If your stress level per day was high, try to spend more time sleeping. it is the sleep that contributes to our weight loss and getting rid of all diseases. There are some tips to improve your sleep comfort:

- Keep cool in the room. The optimum temperature should not exceed 65-70F.
- Use a black mask for sleeping and earplugs.
- Provide good room ventilation.

7. Don't forget about vegetables.

It is obvious that the main resource of vitamins and minerals is vegetables. You can't cross out them totally from daily meals. Consuming them during the keto diet is very important, but should be in moderation. Starchy vegetables such as sweet potatoes and potatoes are not allowed. Nevertheless, at the same time, you can safely substitute them with broccoli, kale, spinach, white cabbage, Brussels sprouts to your diet. Such vegetables are not only low-carb, but also low-calorie and have a huge number of vitamins, antioxidants, and minerals. They will help you stay full for a long time and protect from eating an extra serving of nuts.

One of the tips of keto coaches is to pamper yourself with low-carb berries once a week. At the same time, it is very important to increase physical activity during this day. Cycling will be just right. All this will fill your body with useful antioxidants and will not add extra pounds.

8. MCT oil is a treasure for a keto diet.

MCT oil is medium-chain triglyceride oil. It practically doesn't require splitting in the small intestine and is absorbed already in the duodenum, going directly to the liver. MCT oil is used by the body as an energy source, which leads to an increase in fat loss. On the other hand, MCT oil isn't deposited in body fat like fatty tissue in comparison with other fatty acids, and it has been shown that it improves thermogenesis, that is, the process during which the body creates heat using excess energy.

MCT oils are good for cooking, especially for baking, frying or grilling. This is due to their high point of "smoke", which means that they are very difficult to oxidize from heat and can withstand high temperatures without losing their original chemical structure at room temperature (losing their useful properties). You can also add MTC oil in keto shakes, coffee, tea, and other keto drinks.

9.   Do a kitchen audit

The key to getting ketosis is proper low-carb nutrition. Nevertheless, our brain, knowing that somewhere in the fridge or freezer are a bar of chocolate or a package of vanilla ice cream. So it unconsciously creates situations in which we are obliged to eat them. That's why there are no doubts that one of the best tips is to clean your kitchen and all the shelves from the "seducers". Firstly, write a list of food that is not allowed during the diet, and then one by one throw away everything that is on your list. It may seem too radical right away. But just know that all this will help you completely switch to keto life faster and less stressfully for your body. Also, you can make a list of all you have in the fridge and stick this sheet of paper on the fridge. Doing this you will not eat extra snacks during the day.

10.   Keep food near you.

Our life is full of events and sometimes we just don't have time to cook. We have a choice to buy high carbohydrate food in the shop or cook the right food by ourselves. All of this needs extra time. That's why you should always have a "healthy snack" with you. No matter what it is. It can be fat bombs, seeds, or nuts. If you have more time, make the keto salads, or find the keto fruits such as avocado and cook the spreads and dips. But bear in mind, you shouldn't cook much in advance. Their expired date is very short. Follow the rule to purchasing all ingredients for snacks in advance, so that they are always in your fridge. This way you can less likely break your diet and get rid of unnecessary overeating. If you don't know what to cook, use the recipe generator which can help you with the meal for your certain list of food.

BREAKFAST

Breakfast Casserole

Prep time: 10 minutes | **Cook time:** 20 minutes | **Yield:** 6 servings

Ingredients

1 cup ground chicken

1 cup Cheddar cheese, shredded

½ cup coconut cream

1 teaspoon salt

1 teaspoon chili flakes

1 teaspoon olive oil

Method

1. Preheat the instant pot on Manual mode for 3 minutes.

2. Then add olive oil, ground chicken, salt, and chili flakes.

3. Cook the ground chicken on Saute mode for 10 minutes.

4. Then stir it well and add coconut cream and Cheddar cheese.

5. Close the lid and cook the casserole on Manual mode (high pressure) for 10 minutes. Then make a quick pressure release and let the meal cool for 10 minutes.

Nutritional info per serve: calories 173, fat 13.5, fiber 0.4, carbs 1.4, protein 11.9

Eggs Benedict

Prep time: 10 minutes | **Cook time:** 1 minute | **Yield:** 3 servings

Ingredients

3 eggs

3 turkey bacon slices, fried

1 teaspoon butter

½ teaspoon ground black pepper

1 cup of water

¼ teaspoon salt

Method

1. Grease the eggs molds with butter and crack eggs inside.

2. Sprinkle them with ground black pepper and salt.

3. Pour water in the instant pot and insert the rack.

4. Then place the eggs in the molds in the rack and close the lid.

5. Cook the eggs for 1 minute on Manual mode (high pressure).

6. Then make a quick pressure release and transfer the eggs on the plate.

7. Top the eggs with bacon slices.

Nutritional info per serve: calories 95, fat 6.2, fiber 0.1, carbs 0.6, protein 8.6

Starbucks Eggs

Prep time: 10 minutes | **Cook time:** 2 minutes | **Yield:** 2 servings

Ingredients

4 eggs

2 oz cottage cheese

1/3 cup Cheddar cheese, shredded

1 teaspoon chives, chopped

1 cup of water

Method

1. Crack the eggs in the bowl and mix them with chives.

2. Whisk the eggs and add shredded Cheddar cheese and cottage cheese. Stir well.

3. Then pour the eggs in the muffin molds.

4. Pour water in the instant pot and insert the steamer rack.

5. Place the eggs on the rack and cook them for 2 minutes on Manual mode (high pressure).

6. Make a quick pressure release and remove the eggs from the molds.

Nutritional info per serve: calories 227, fat 15.5, fiber 0, carbs 2, protein 19.7

Frittata with Greens

Prep time: 10 minutes | **Cook time:** 10 minutes | **Yield:** 2 servings

Ingredients

2 eggs, beaten

¼ cup heavy cream

½ teaspoon white pepper

1 tablespoon chives, chopped

1 teaspoon ground paprika

1 teaspoon butter, softened

1 tablespoon scallions, chopped

1 cup water, for cooking

Method

1. In the mixing bowl, mix up eggs, heavy cream, white pepper, chives, ground paprika, and scallions.

2. Then grease the frittata ramekin with softened butter.

3. Pour the egg mixture in the prepared ramekin and place it on the trivet.

4. Then pour water in the instant pot and insert the trivet inside.

5. Cook the frittata for 10 minutes on Manual mode (high pressure).

6. Then make a quick pressure release and cut the meal into halves.

Nutritional info per serve: calories 137, fat 12, fiber 0.7, carbs 2, protein 6.2

Egg Cups

Prep time: 15 minutes | **Cook time:** 13 minutes | **Yield:** 4 servings

Ingredients

4 eggs

¼ cups spinach, chopped

½ teaspoon chili flakes

2 oz Mozzarella, sliced

1 teaspoon butter, melted

1 cup water, for cooking

Method

1. Brush the muffin molds with butter.

2. Then crack the egg in every mold and sprinkle them with chili flakes and spinach.

3. Top the eggs with sliced Mozzarella.

4. Pour water and insert the steamer rack in the instant pot.

5. Put the egg cups on the rack and close the lid.

6. Cook the meal on manual mode (high pressure) for 3 minutes. Make a quick pressure release.

7. Let the cooked egg cups cool to room temperature. Remove the eggs from the muffin molds.

Nutritional info per serve: calories 112, fat 7.8, fiber 0, carbs 0.9, protein 9.6

Bacon and Cheese Bites

Prep time: 15 minutes | **Cook time:** 3 minutes | **Yield:** 2 servings

Ingredients

2 tablespoons coconut flour

½ cup Cheddar cheese, shredded

2 teaspoons coconut cream

2 bacon slices, cooked

½ teaspoon dried parsley

1 cup water, for cooking

Method

1. In the mixing bowl, mix up coconut flour, Cheddar cheese, coconut cream, and dried parsley.

2. Then chop the cooked bacon and add it in the mixture.

3. Stir it well.

4. Pour water and insert the trivet in the instant pot.

5. Line the trivet with baking paper.

6. After this, make the small balls (bites) from the cheese mixture and put them on the prepared trivet.

7. Cook the meal for 3 minutes on manual mode (high pressure).

8. Then make a quick pressure release and cool the cooked meal well.

Nutritional info per serve: calories 258, fat 19.2, fiber 3.1, carbs 5.9, protein 15.2

Noatmeal

Prep time: 10 minutes | **Cook time:** 5 hours | **Yield:** 4 servings

Ingredients

½ cup coconut shred

1 teaspoon ground cinnamon

1 teaspoon Erythritol

3 tablespoons flaxseeds

3 tablespoons sunflower seeds

½ cup coconut cream

½ cup of water

½ teaspoon butter

Method

1. In the mixing bowl, mix up coconut shred, ground cinnamon, Erythritol, flaxseeds, sunflower seeds, coconut cream, water, and butter.

2. Transfer the mixture in the instant pot bowl.

3. Set the slow cook mode and cook the meal for 5 hours.

4. Then stir it well and transfer in the serving ramekins.

Nutritional info per serve: calories 215, fat 20.4, fiber 4.6, carbs 8.1, protein 2.1

Breakfast Sandwich

Prep time: 10 minutes | **Cook time:** 15 minutes | **Yield:** 4 servings

Ingredients

1 cup lettuce

2 cups ground chicken

1 tablespoon coconut flour

1 teaspoon salt

1 tablespoon butter

½ teaspoon ground nutmeg

3 oz scallions, chopped

Method

1.   Preheat the instant pot on saute mode for 5 minutes.

2.   Then add butter and melt it.

3.   Add chopped scallions

4.   After this, add ground chicken and ground nutmeg. Stir the mixture well and cook for 4 minutes.

5.   Then add coconut flour and salt. Saute the meal for 10 minutes.

6.   Fill the lettuce with the ground chicken and transfer it on the plate. The sandwiches are cooked.

Nutritional info per serve: calories 177, fat 8.6, fiber 1.5, carbs 3.2, protein 21.1

Morning Burritos

Prep time: 10 minutes | **Cook time:** 15 minutes | **Yield:** 4 servings

Ingredients

4 keto tortillas

1 cup ground beef

¼ cup crushed tomatoes

1 teaspoon olive oil

3 oz scallions, diced

½ teaspoon dried cilantro

Method

1.   In the mixing bowl mix up ground beef, crushed tomatoes, olive oil, scallions, and dried cilantro.

2.   Put the meat mixture in the instant pot.

3.   Close and seal the lid.

4.   Cook the beef mixture for 15 minutes on Manual mode (high pressure).

5.   Then make a quick pressure release and stir the meat well.

6.   Fill the tortillas with the cooked mixture and roll them in the shape of burritos.

Nutritional info per serve: calories 238, fat 13.3, fiber 5.1, carbs 10.8, protein 19.3

White Cabbage Hash Browns

Prep time: 10 minutes | **Cook time:** 10 minutes | **Yield:** 3 servings

Ingredients

1 cup white cabbage, shredded

3 eggs, beaten

½ teaspoon ground nutmeg

½ teaspoon salt

1 tablespoon coconut oil

½ teaspoon onion powder

½ zucchini, grated

Method

1. In the mixing bowl, mix up shredded cabbage, eggs, ground nutmeg, salt, onion powder, and grated zucchini.

2. Then heat up coconut oil in the instant pot on Saute mode.

3. Make the medium hash browns from the cabbage mixture (use the tablespoon for this step).

4. After this, place the hash browns in the hot coconut oil.

5. Cook them on saute mode for 4 minutes from each side.

Nutritional info per serve: calories 116, fat 9.1, fiber 1, carbs 3.3, protein 6.3

Giant Vanilla Pancake

Prep time: 15 minutes | **Cook time:** 50 minutes | **Yield:** 6 servings

Ingredients

½ cup coconut flour

3 tablespoons swerve

¼ cup heavy cream

3 eggs, beaten

1 teaspoon vanilla extract

¼ cup almond flour

1 teaspoon baking powder

Cooking spray

Method

1. In the mixing bowl, mix up coconut flour, swerve, heavy cream, eggs, vanilla extract, and almond flour.

2. Then add baking powder and whisk the mixture until smooth.

3. Pour the pancake mixture in the instant pot.

4. Cook the meal on manual mode (low pressure) for 50 minutes.

Nutritional info per serve: calories 122, fat 7.3, fiber 4.5, carbs 9.5, protein 5.2

Meat Cups

Prep time: 15 minutes | **Cook time:** 15 minutes | **Yield:** 4 servings

Ingredients

4 quill eggs

10 oz ground pork

1 jalapeno pepper, chopped

½ teaspoon salt

1 teaspoon dried dill

1 tablespoon butter, softened

1 cup water, for cooking

Method

1. In the mixing bowl, mix up ground pork, chopped jalapeno pepper, salt, dill, and butter.

2. When the meat mixture is homogenous, transfer it in the silicone muffin molds and press the surface gently.

3. Then pour water in the instant pot and insert the trivet.

4. Place the meat cups on the trivet.

5. Then crack the eggs over the meat mixture and close the lid.

6. Cook the meal on manual mode (high pressure) for 15 minutes.

7. Then make a quick pressure release.

Nutritional info per serve: calories 143, fat 6.4, fiber 0.1, carbs 0.4, protein 19.9

Bell Peppers with Omelet

Prep time: 10 minutes | **Cook time:** 14 minutes | **Yield:** 2 servings

Ingredients

1 large bell pepper

2 eggs, beaten

1 tablespoon coconut cream

¼ teaspoon salt

¼ teaspoon dried oregano

1 cup of water

Method

1. Cut the bell peppers into halves and remove the seeds.

2. After this, in the mixing bowl mix up eggs, coconut cream, salt, and oregano.

3. Pour water in the instant pot and insert the rack.

4. Then pour the egg mixture in the pepper halves.

5. Transfer the peppers on the rack and close the lid.

6. Cook the meal on Manual mode (high pressure) for 14 minutes. Then make a quick pressure release.

Nutritional info per serve: calories 100, fat 6.3, fiber 1.1, carbs 5.4, protein 6.3

Bacon Avocado Bomb

Prep time: 10 minutes | **Cook time:** 25 minutes | **Yield:** 4 servings

Ingredients

1 avocado, pilled, pitted, halved

4 bacon slices

½ teaspoon ground cinnamon

1 teaspoon coconut cream

½ teaspoon chili flakes

Method

1. Sprinkle the avocado with ground cinnamon and chili flakes.

2. Then fill it with coconut cream and wrap in the bacon slices.

3. Secure the avocado bomb with toothpicks, if needed and wrap in the foil.

4. Place it in the instant pot and close the lid.

5. Cook the bomb on saute mode for 25 minutes.

6. Then remove the foil and slice the avocado bomb into the servings.

Nutritional info per serve: calories 209, fat 18, fiber 3.6, carbs 4.9, protein 8

Stuffed Hard-Boiled Eggs

Prep time: 10 minutes | **Cook time:** 5 minutes | **Yield:** 6 servings

Ingredients

6 eggs

3 oz Provolone cheese, grated

1 teaspoon chili pepper, chopped

1 tablespoon coconut cream

½ teaspoon ground paprika

1 cup of water

Method

1. Pour water in the instant pot.

2. Add eggs and close the lid.

3. Cook the on manual mode (high pressure) for 5 minutes. Then allow the natural pressure release and open the lid.

4. Cool and peel the eggs.

5. After this, cut the eggs into halves and remove the egg yolks.

6. Mash the egg yolks and mix them up with grated cheese, coconut cream, chili pepper, and ground paprika.

7. Then fill the egg white halves with egg yolk mixture.

Nutritional info per serve: calories 119, fat 8.8, fiber 0.2, carbs 1, protein 9.3

Cheese Roll-Ups

Prep time: 10 minutes | **Cook time:** 5 minutes | **Yield:** 3 servings

Ingredients

3 turkey lunch meat slices

3 oz Parmesan, grated

½ teaspoon minced garlic

1 tablespoon cream cheese

½ teaspoon olive oil

Method

1. Heat up the olive oil on saute mode.

2. Then place the turkey slices in the hot oil and cook them for 2 minutes from each side.

3. Meanwhile, in the mixing bowl mix up cream cheese, minced garlic, and Parmesan.

4. Transfer the cooked turkey slices on the plate and spread them with cheese mixture.

5. Roll up the turkey slices and secure them with the toothpicks.

Nutritional info per serve: calories 160, fat 8, fiber 0, carbs 1.3, protein 21.4

Breakfast Taco Skillet

Prep time: 10 minutes | **Cook time:** 17 minutes | **Yield:** 6 servings

Ingredients

½ avocado, chopped

3 jalapeno peppers, chopped

2 cups ground beef

1 teaspoon chili flakes

1/3 cup coconut milk

¾ cup black olives, sliced

1 teaspoon coconut oil

2 eggs, beaten

Method

1. Melt the coconut oil on saute mode for 2 minutes.

2. Then add ground beef and chili flakes.

3. Cook the meat on saute mode for 4 minutes. Stir it well.

4. Add jalapeno peppers, coconut milk, olives, and eggs,

5. Stir the mixture until homogenous.

6. Add chopped avocado and close the lid.

7. Cook the meal on manual mode (high pressure) for 10 minutes. Then ake the quick pressure release.

Nutritional info per serve: calories 201, fat 16, fiber 2.2, carbs 3.9, protein 11.4

Meat and Cauliflower Bake

Prep time: 10 minutes | **Cook time:** 15 minutes | **Yield:** 4 servings

Ingredients

4 eggs, beaten

1 cup cauliflower, shredded

½ cup ground chicken

1 tablespoon Italian seasonings

½ teaspoon salt

¼ cup Cheddar cheese, shredded

1 cup water, for cooking

Method

1. In the mixing bowl, mix up beaten eggs, shredded cauliflower, Italian seasonings, and salt.
2. Then pour the mixture in 4 ramekins.
3. Add ground chicken.
4. Top the ramekins with Cheddar cheese.
5. Then pour the water in the instant pot, insert the trivet.
6. Put the ramekins on the trivet and close the lid.
7. Cook the meal on manual mode (high pressure) for 15 minutes. Then make a quick pressure release.

Nutritional info per serve: calories 142, fat 9.1, fiber 0.6, carbs 2.1, protein 12.9

Pulled Pork Hash with Eggs

Prep time: 10 minutes | **Cook time:** 15 minutes | **Yield:** 4 servings

Ingredients

4 eggs

10 oz pulled pork, shredded

1 teaspoon coconut oil

1 teaspoon red pepper

1 teaspoon fresh cilantro, chopped

1 tomato, chopped

¼ cup of water

Method

1. Melt the coconut oil in the instant pot on saute mode.
2. Then add pulled pork, red pepper, cilantro, water, and chopped tomato.
3. Cook the ingredients for 5 minutes.
4. Then stir it well with the help of the spatula and crack the eggs over it.
5. Close the lid.
6. Cook the meal on manual mode (high pressure) for 7 minutes. Then make a quick pressure release.

Nutritional info per serve: calories 275, fat 18.3, fiber 0.6, carbs 5.7, protein 22.4

Kale and Eggs Bake

Prep time: 10 minutes | **Cook time:** 10 minutes | **Yield:** 2 servings

Ingredients

½ cup kale, chopped

3 eggs, beaten

1 tablespoon organic almond milk

1 teaspoon coconut oil, melted

¼ teaspoon ground black pepper

1 cup water, for cooking

Method

1. In the mixing bowl, mix up chopped kale, eggs, almond milk, and ground black pepper.

2.   Grease the ramekins with coconut oil.

3.   Pour the kale-egg mixture in the ramekins and flatten it with the help of the spatula, if needed.

4.   Pour water and insert the trivet in the instant pot.

5.   Put the ramekins with egg mixture on the trivet and close the lid.

6.   Cook the breakfast on manual mode (high pressure) for 10 minutes. Make a quick pressure release.

Nutritional info per serve: calories 126, fat 9.1, fiber 0.3, carbs 2.6, protein 8.9

Bacon Casserole

Prep time: 10 minutes | **Cook time:** 10 minutes | **Yield:** 6 servings

Ingredients

4 bacon slices, chopped

1 teaspoon olive oil

6 eggs, beaten

½ cup spinach, chopped

½ cup heavy cream

1 teaspoon chili flakes

3 oz Parmesan, grated

1 teaspoon ground paprika

1 cup water, for cooking

Method

1.   Preheat the instant pot on Saute mode for 2-3 minutes.

2.   Then put the chopped bacon inside and cook it on saute mode for 5 minutes or until it is crunchy.

3.   Then transfer the cooked bacon in the mixing bowl. Add the eggs, spinach, heavy cream, chili flakes, paprika, and Parmesan. Carefully stir the. Clean the instant pot and pour water and insert the steamer rack inside.

4.   After this, pour the mixture in the baking mold/ramekin and cover with foil. Cook the casserole on manual (high pressure) for 15 minutes. Allow the natural pressure release for 10 minutes.

Nutritional info per serve: calories 220, fat 17.2, fiber 0.2, carbs 1.6, protein 15.1

Swedish Meatballs

Prep time: 15 minutes | **Cook time:** 25 minutes | **Yield:** 2 servings

Ingredients

1/3 cup ground beef

¼ cup ground pork

¼ teaspoon white pepper

1 teaspoon avocado oil

½ teaspoon ground black pepper

1 teaspoon coconut flour

¼ teaspoon Erythritol

½ cup coconut cream

Method

1.   In the mixing bowl, mix up ground beef, ground pork, white pepper, ground black pepper, and Erythritol.

2.   Make the small meatballs.

3.   Preheat the instant pot on saute mode for 2 minutes and add avocado oil.

4.   Put the meatballs in the hot oil in one layer and cook them for 3 minutes from each side.

5. Meanwhile, mix up coconut cream and coconut flour.

6. Pour the liquid over the meatballs and close the lid. Cook the meal on saute mode for 15 minutes.

Nutritional info per serve: calories 331, fat 26.5, fiber 4, carbs 8.3, protein 16.8

Egg Cups on the Run

Prep time: 10 minutes | **Cook time:** 6 minutes | **Yield:** 3 servings

Ingredients

3 eggs, beaten

1 oz tomato, chopped

1 oz celery stalk, chopped

1 tablespoon chives, chopped

3 oz Cheddar cheese, shredded

½ cup heavy cream

¼ teaspoon chili powder

1 cup water, for cooking

Method

1. In the mixing bowl, mix up eggs, tomato, celery stalk, chives, cheese, heavy cream, and chili powder.

2. Then pour the mixture in the glass cups.

3. Pour water and insert the steamer rack in the instant pot.

4. Then place the glass cups with egg mixture on the rack. Close and seal the lid.

5. Cook the meal on manual (high pressure) for 6 minutes. Make a quick pressure release.

Nutritional info per serve: calories 250, fat 21.3, fiber 0.4, carbs 2.1, protein 13.2

Margherita Egg Cups

Prep time: 10 minutes | **Cook time:** 5 minutes | **Yield:** 2 servings

Ingredients

2 eggs

4 oz Mozzarella, shredded

½ tomato, chopped

1 teaspoon butter, softened

½ teaspoon fresh basil, chopped

1 cup water, for cooking

Method

1. Grease the small ramekins with softened butter and crack the eggs inside.

2. Then top the eggs with chopped tomato, basil, and Mozzarella.

3. Pour water and insert the steamer rack in the instant pot.

4. Place the ramekins with eggs on the rack. Close and seal the lid.

5. Cook the meal on manual (high pressure) for 5 minutes. Allow the natural pressure release for 5 minutes.

Nutritional info per serve: calories 243, fat 16.3, fiber 0.2, carbs 3, protein 21.7

APPETIZERS AND SIDES

Cauliflower Queso

Prep time: 10 minutes | **Cook time:** 30 minutes | **Yield:** 5 servings

Ingredients

2 cups cauliflower, chopped

1/3 cup cream cheese

½ cup Cheddar cheese

1 jalapeno, chopped

2 oz scallions, diced

1 tablespoon nutritional yeast

1 tablespoon olive oil

2 garlic cloves, diced

Method

1. Put chopped cauliflower, cream cheese, Cheddar cheese, jalapeno, diced scallions, nutritional yeast, olive oil, and diced garlic clove.

2. Stir the mixture well with the help of the spoon and close the lid.

3. Cook the queso for 30 minutes on saute mode. Stir meal every 5 minutes to avoid burning.

Nutritional info per serve: calories 146, fat 12.1, fiber 1.9, carbs 5, protein 6

Sweet Smokies

Prep time: 5 minutes | **Cook time:** 15 minutes | **Yield:** 3 servings

Ingredients

1 teaspoon Erythritol

½ teaspoon sesame seeds

2 tablespoons keto BBQ sauce

8 oz cocktail sausages

1/3 cup chicken broth

Method

1. Put Erythritol, sesame seeds, BBQ sauce, and chicken broth in the instant pot.

2. Preheat the mixture on saute mode for 2 minutes.

3. Then add cocktail sausages and stir the mixture well.

4. Cook the meal for 10 minutes on saute mode. Stir the sausages every 2 minutes.

Nutritional info per serve: calories 49, fat 2.5, fiber 5.7, carbs 0.1, protein 2.3

Rosemary Chicken Wings

Prep time: 10 minutes | **Cook time:** 16 minutes | **Yield:** 4 servings

Ingredients

4 chicken wings, boneless

1 tablespoon olive oil

1 teaspoon dried rosemary

½ teaspoon garlic powder

¼ teaspoon salt

Method

1. In the mixing bowl, mix up olive oil, dried rosemary, garlic powder, and salt.

2. Then rub the chicken wings with the rosemary mixture and leave for 10 minutes to marinate.

3. After this, put the chicken wings in the instant pot, add the remaining rosemary

marinade and cook them on saute mode for 8 minutes from each side.

Nutritional info per serve: calories 222, fat 11.1, fiber 0.2, carbs 1.8, protein 27.5

Classic Meatballs

Prep time: 20 minutes | **Cook time:** 15 minutes | **Yield:** 6 servings

Ingredients

7 oz ground beef

7 oz ground pork

1 teaspoon minced garlic

3 tablespoons water

1 teaspoon chili flakes

1 teaspoon dried parsley

1 tablespoon coconut oil

¼ cup beef broth

Method

1.   In the mixing bowl, mix up ground beef, ground pork, minced garlic, water, chili flakes, and dried parsley.

2.   Make the medium size meatballs from the mixture.

3.   After this, heat up coconut oil in the instant pot on saute mode.

4.   Put the meatballs in the hot coconut oil in one layer and cook them for 2 minutes from each side.

5.   Then add beef broth and close the lid.

6.   Cook the meatballs for 10 minutes on manual mode (high pressure).

7.   Then make a quick pressure release and transfer the meatballs on the plate.

Nutritional info per serve: calories 131, fat 5.6, fiber 0, carbs 0.2, protein 18.9

Bacon Deviled Eggs

Prep time: 10 minutes | **Cook time:** 15 minutes | **Yield:** 4 servings

Ingredients

2 eggs

1 teaspoon cream cheese

1 oz Parmesan, grated

¼ teaspoon red pepper

1 oz bacon, chopped

1 cup of water

Method

1.   Pour water in the instant pot.

2.   Add eggs and cook them for 5 minutes on manual mode (high pressure).

3.   Then make a quick pressure release. Cool and peel the eggs.

4.   After this, clean the instant pot bowl and put the bacon inside.

5.   Cook it on saute mode for 10 minutes. Stir it from time to time to avoid burning.

6.   Cut the eggs into halves.

7.   Put the egg yolks in the bowl and smash them with the help of the fork.

8.   Add red pepper, cooked bacon, and cream cheese. Mix up the mixture.

9.   Then fill the egg whites with the bacon mixture.

Nutritional info per serve: calories 98, fat 7, fiber 0.1, carbs 1.1, protein 7.8

Spinach Dip

Prep time: 10 minutes | **Cook time:** 6 hours | **Yield:** 4 servings

Ingredients

2 cups spinach, chopped

1 cup Mozzarella, shredded

2 artichoke hearts, chopped

1 teaspoon ground ginger

1 teaspoon butter

½ teaspoon white pepper

½ cup heavy cream

Method

1.   Put the spinach, artichoke hearts, and butter in the instant pot bowl.

2.   Add Mozzarella, ground ginger, white pepper, and heavy cream. Stir the mixture gently.

3.   Cook it in manual mode (Low pressure) for 6 hours. Then stir well and transfer in the serving bowl.

Nutritional info per serve: calories 124, fat 8, fiber 4.8, carbs 10.2, protein 5.5

Sausage Balls

Prep time: 10 minutes | **Cook time:** 16 minutes | **Yield:** 10 servings

Ingredients

15 oz ground pork sausage

1 teaspoon dried oregano

4 oz Mozzarella, shredded

1 cup coconut flour

1 garlic clove, grated

1 teaspoon coconut oil, melted

Method

1.   In the bowl mix up ground pork sausages, dried oregano, shredded Mozzarella, coconut flour, and garlic clove.

2.   When the mixture is homogenous, make the balls.

3.   After this, pour coconut oil in the instant pot.

4.   Arrange the balls in the instant pot and cook them on saute mode for 8 minutes from each side.

Nutritional info per serve: calories 310, fat 23.2, fiber 4.9, carbs 10.1, protein 16.8

BLT Dip

Prep time: 10 minutes | **Cook time:** 20 minutes | **Yield:** 3 servings

Ingredients

2 teaspoons cream cheese

3 oz bacon, chopped

2 tablespoons sour cream

2 oz Cheddar cheese, shredded

¼ teaspoon minced garlic

1 teaspoon smoked paprika

1 tomato, chopped

¼ cup lettuce, chopped

Method

1.   Preheat the instant pot on saute mode.

2.   Put the chopped bacon in the instant pot and cook it for 5 minutes. Stir it from time to time.

3.   Then add cream cheese, sour cream, Cheddar cheese, garlic, smoked paprika, and tomato.

4. Close the lid and cook the dip on saute mode for 15 minutes.

5. Then stir it well and mix up with lettuce.

Nutritional info per serve: calories 261, fat 20.7, fiber 0.5, carbs 2.5, protein 15.9

Taco Bites

Prep time: 10 minutes | **Cook time:** 15 minutes | **Yield:** 6 servings

Ingredients

10 oz ground beef

3 eggs, beaten

1/3 cup Mozzarella, shredded

1 teaspoon taco seasoning

1 teaspoon sesame oil

Method

1. In the mixing bowl mix up ground beef, eggs, Mozzarella, and taco seasoning.

2. Then make the small meat bites from the mixture.

3. Heat up sesame oil in the instant pot.

4. Put the meat bites in the hot oil and cook them for 5 minutes from each side on Saute mode.

Nutritional info per serve: calories 132, fat 6.2, fiber 0, carbs 0.6, protein 17.5

Sausage Dip

Prep time: 10 minutes | **Cook time:** 25 minutes | **Yield:** 7 servings

Ingredients

12 oz Italian sausages

1 chili pepper, chopped

5 oz Cheddar cheese, shredded

1 teaspoon coconut oil

1 teaspoon tomato paste

¼ cup heavy cream

Method

1. Heat up coconut oil in the instant pot.

2. Then add Italian sausages and cook them on Saute mode for 10 minutes. Mix up the sausages every 3 minutes.

3. Then add chili pepper, shredded Cheddar cheese, tomato paste, and heavy cream.

4. Close the lid and cook the dip on manual mode (high pressure) for 10 minutes. Make a quick pressure release.

Nutritional info per serve: calories 271, fat 24.2, fiber 0.1, carbs 0.9, protein 12.1

Stuffed Mushrooms

Prep time: 15 minutes | **Cook time:** 8 minutes | **Yield:** 4 servings

Ingredients

1 cup cremini mushroom caps

1 tablespoon scallions, chopped

1 tablespoon chives, chopped

1 teaspoon cream cheese

1 teaspoon sour cream

1 oz Monterey Jack cheese, shredded

1 teaspoon butter, softened

½ teaspoon smoked paprika

1 cup water, for cooking

Method

1. Trim the mushroom caps if needed and wash them well.

2. After this, in the mixing bowl, mix up scallions, chives, cream cheese, sour cream, butter, and smoked paprika.

3. Then fill the mushroom caps with the cream cheese mixture and top with shredded Monterey Jack cheese.

4. Pour water and insert the trivet in the instant pot.

5. Arrange the stuffed mushrooms caps on the trivet and close the lid.

6. Cook the meal on Manual (high pressure) for 8 minutes.

7. Then make a quick pressure release.

Nutritional info per serve: calories 45, fat 3.7, fiber 0.3, carbs 1, protein 2.5

Cheese Jalapenos

Prep time: 10 minutes | **Cook time:** 7 minutes | **Yield:** 4 servings

Ingredients

4 jalapeno peppers

1 egg, beaten

½ cup Monterey Jack cheese, shredded

1 teaspoon almond butter, softened

1 cup water, for cooking

Method

1. Cut the jalapenos into halves and remove the seeds.

2. In the mixing bowl, mix up softened almond butter, cheese, and egg.

3. Then fill the jalapeno halves with cheese mixture.

4. Put the jalapenos in the ramekin.

5. Then pour water and insert the rack in the instant pot.

6. Put the ramekin with jalapenos on the rack and close the lid.

7. Cook the meal for 7 minutes on manual (high pressure). Make a quick pressure release.

Nutritional info per serve: calories 99, fat 7.8, fiber 1, carbs 2, protein 5.9

Coconut Shrimps

Prep time: 10 minutes | **Cook time:** 6 minutes | **Yield:** 2 servings

Ingredients

4 Royal tiger shrimps

3 tablespoons coconut shred

2 eggs, beaten

½ teaspoon Cajun seasonings

1 teaspoon olive oil

Method

1. Heat up olive oil in the instant pot on saute mode.

2. Meanwhile, mix up Cajun seasonings and coconut shred.

3. Dip the shrimps in the eggs and coat in the coconut shred mixture.

4. After this, place the shrimps in the hot olive oil and cook them on saute mode for 3 minutes from each side.

Nutritional info per serve: calories 292, fat 53.7, fiber 1, carbs 2.3, protein 40.1

Scallion Dip

Prep time: 10 minutes | **Cook time:** 11 minutes | **Yield:** 4 servings

Ingredients

5 oz scallions, diced

4 tablespoons cream cheese

1 tablespoon fresh parsley, chopped

1 teaspoon garlic powder

2 tablespoons coconut cream

½ teaspoon salt

1 teaspoon coconut oil

Method

1.   Heat up the instant pot on saute mode.

2.   Then add coconut oil and melt it.

3.   Add diced scallions and saute it for 6-7 minutes or until it is light brown.

4.   Add cream cheese, parsley, garlic powder, salt, and coconut cream.

5.   Close the instant pot lid and cook the scallions dip for 5 minutes on Manual mode (high pressure).

6.   Make a quick pressure release. Blend the dip will it is smooth if desired.

Nutritional info per serve: calories 76, fat 6.5, fiber 1.2, carbs 3.9, protein 1.7

Eggplant Bites

Prep time: 15 minutes | **Cook time:** 20 minutes | **Yield:** 4 servings

Ingredients

1 teaspoon minced garlic

1 tablespoon apple cider vinegar

1 tablespoon sesame oil

1 teaspoon salt

2 large eggplants, trimmed

1 teaspoon dried sage

Method

1.   Slice the eggplants and rub them with salt.

2.   After this, in the shallow bowl mix up minced garlic, apple cider vinegar, sesame oil, and dried sage.

3.   Then rub every eggplant slice with a minced garlic mixture.

4.   Heat up the instant pot on saute mode.

5.   Then place the eggplant slices in the instant pot in one layer. Cook the vegetables for 2 minutes from each side or until the eggplants are tender.

Nutritional info per serve: calories 101, fat 3.9, fiber 9.8, carbs 16.5, protein 2.8

Bacon Peppers

Prep time: 15 minutes | **Cook time:** 6 minutes | **Yield:** 2 servings

Ingredients

2 jalapenos

1 oz bacon, chopped, fried

1 teaspoon green onions, chopped

1 tablespoon coconut cream

2 oz Cheddar cheese, shredded

Method

1.   Trim the jalapenos and remove the seeds.

2.   In the mixing bowl, mix up chopped bacon, green onions, coconut cream, and shredded cheese.

3.   Fill the jalapenos with the bacon mixture.

4.   Heat up the instant pot on saute mode for 5 minutes.

5.   Put the jalapenos in the instant pot and cook them for 3 minutes from each side.

Nutritional info per serve: calories 213, fat 17.2, fiber 0.6, carbs 1.9, protein 12.7

Fat Bombs

Prep time: 10 minutes | **Cook time:** 10 minutes | **Yield:** 3 servings

Ingredients

3 eggs

3 bacon slices

½ teaspoon cayenne pepper

2 tablespoons cream cheese

½ teaspoon salt

Method

1.   Put the bacon in the instant pot and cook it on saute mode for 3 minutes from each side.

2.   Then chop the bacon and put it in the bowl.

3.   Crack the eggs in the instant pot and whisk gently.

4.   Cook the eggs for 5 minutes on manual mode (high pressure). Make a quick pressure release.

5.   Then transfer the cooked eggs in the bowl with bacon and shred.

6.   Add cayenne pepper, cream cheese, and salt. Stir well.

7.   Make the medium size bombs.

Nutritional info per serve: calories 190, fat 14.7, fiber 0.1, carbs 1, protein 13.1

Chicken Celery Sticks

Prep time: 15 minutes | **Cook time:** 15 minutes | **Yield:** 4 servings

Ingredients

14 oz chicken breast, skinless, boneless

1 cup of water

1 teaspoon salt

½ teaspoon onion powder

4 celery stalks

1 teaspoon Keto mayo

Method

1.   Put the chicken breast in the instant pot.

2.   Add water, salt, and onion powder.

3.   Cook the chicken on manual mode (high pressure) for 15 minutes. Allow the natural pressure release for 6 minutes.

4.   Remove the cooked chicken from the instant pot and shred it.

5.   Add Keto mayo and stir well.

6.   Fill the celery stalks with shredded chicken.

Nutritional info per serve: calories 118, fat 2.6, fiber 0.3, carbs 0.9, protein 21.2

Reuben Pickles

Prep time: 20 minutes | **Cook time:** 2 hours | **Yield:** 6 servings

Ingredients

1-pound corned beef brisket

2 cups of water

1 cup pickled cucumbers

2 oz provolone cheese, sliced

Method

1.   Put corned beef brisket and water in the instant pot.

2. Cook the meat on manual mode (high pressure) for 2 hours. Allow the natural pressure release for 10 minutes.

3. Then remove the meat from water and slice it.

4. Make the Reuben pickles: pin the meat piece, pickled cucumber, and provolone cheese together to get the small bites.

Nutritional info per serve: calories 164, fat 12, fiber 0.1, carbs 0.8, protein 12.7

Parmesan Balls with Greens

Prep time: 10 minutes | **Cook time:** 20 minutes | **Yield:** 4 servings

Ingredients

3 oz Parmesan, grated

1 cup ground chicken

1 tablespoon chives, chopped

1 teaspoon cayenne pepper

¼ cup chicken broth

1 teaspoon coconut oil, softened

Method

1. Heat up coconut oil in the instant pot on saute mode.

2. Add ground chicken, cayenne pepper, chives, and chicken broth.

3. Close the lid and cook the chicken on manual mode (high pressure) for 15 minutes.

4. Then make a quick pressure release and open the lid.

5. Add Parmesan and stir the chicken mixture well.

6. Make the balls from the cooked mixture and cool them for 10 minutes before serving.

Nutritional info per serve: calories 149, fat 8.5, fiber 0.1, carbs 1.1, protein 17.3

Cheese Stuffed Shishito Peppers

Prep time: 20 minutes | **Cook time:** 7 minutes | **Yield:** 4 servings

Ingredients

8 oz shishito peppers

1 cup Cheddar cheese, shredded

4 tablespoons cream cheese

1 tablespoon fresh parsley, chopped

¼ teaspoon minced garlic

1 tablespoon butter, melted

1 cup water, for cooking

Method

1. Cut the ends of the peppers and remove the seeds.

2. After this, in the mixing bowl mix up shredded cheese, cream cheese, parsley, and minced garlic.

3. Then fill the peppers with cheese mixture and put in the baking mold.

4. Sprinkle the peppers with melted butter.

5. After this, pour water and insert the steamer rack.

6. Place the mold with peppers on the rack. Close and seal the lid.

7. Cook the meal on manual (high pressure) for 7 minutes. Allow the natural pressure release for 5 minutes.

Nutritional info per serve: calories 194, fat 15.7, fiber 2.6, carbs 4.5, protein 9.1

Roasted Tomatillos

Prep time: 10 minutes | **Cook time:** 10 minutes | **Yield:** 4 servings

Ingredients

1 tablespoon Italian seasonings

4 tomatillos, sliced

4 teaspoons olive oil

4 tablespoons water

Method

1.   Sprinkle the tomatillos with Italian seasoning.

2.   Then pour the olive oil in the instant pot and heat it up on saute mode for 1 minute.

3.   Put the tomatillos in the instant pot in one layer and cook them for 2 minutes from each side.

4.   Then add water and close the lid.

5.   Saute the vegetables for 3 minutes more.

Nutritional info per serve: calories 51, fat 5, fiber 0.7, carbs 2, protein 0.3

Chicken&Chinese Cabbage Salad

Prep time: 15 minutes | **Cook time:** 10 minutes | **Yield:** 4 servings

Ingredients

12 oz chicken fillet, chopped

1 teaspoon Cajun seasonings

1 tablespoon coconut oil

1 cup Chinese cabbage, chopped

1 tablespoon avocado oil

1 teaspoon sesame seeds

Method

1.   Sprinkle the chopped chicken with Cajun seasonings and put in the instant pot.

2.   Add coconut oil and cook the chicken on saute mode for 10 minutes. Stir it from time to time with the help of a spatula.

3.   When the chicken is cooked, transfer it in the salad bowl.

4.   Add Chinese cabbage, avocado oil, and sesame seeds.

5.   Mix up the salad.

Nutritional info per serve: calories 202, fat 10.6, fiber 0.4, carbs 0.8, protein 25

Cauliflower Fritters

Prep time: 10 minutes | **Cook time:** 10 minutes | **Yield:** 4 servings

Ingredients

1 cup cauliflower, boiled

2 oz Cheddar cheese, shredded

2 tablespoons almond flour

½ teaspoon garlic powder

2 eggs, beaten

1 tablespoon avocado oil

Method

1.   Mash the cauliflower and mix it up with Cheddar cheese, almond flour, garlic powder, and eggs.

2.   Heat up the avocado oil on saute mode for 1 minute.

3.   Meanwhile, make the fritters from the cauliflower mixture.

4.   Put them in the hot oil and cook for 3 minutes from each side.

Nutritional info per serve: calories 122, fat 9, fiber 1.2, carbs 2.9, protein 7.7

Zucchini Cheese Tots

Prep time: 15 minutes | **Cook time:** 10 minutes | **Yield:** 6 servings

Ingredients

4 oz Parmesan, grated

4 oz Cheddar cheese, grated

1 zucchini, grated

1 egg, beaten

1 teaspoon dried oregano

1 tablespoon coconut oil

Method

1.   In the mixing bowl, mix up Parmesan, Cheddar cheese, zucchini, egg, and dried oregano.

2.   Make the small tots with the help of the fingertips.

3.   Then melt the coconut oil in the instant pot on saute mode.

4.   Put the prepared zucchini tots in the hot coconut oil and cook them for 3 minutes from each side or until they are light brown.

5.   Cool the zucchini tots for 5 minutes.

Nutritional info per serve: calories 173, fat 13.4, fiber 0.5, carbs 2.2, protein 12.1

Red Cauliflower Rice

Prep time: 10 minutes | **Cook time:** 3 minutes | **Yield:** 4 servings

Ingredients

1 cup cauliflower, shredded

1 teaspoon tomato paste

½ cup coconut cream

½ teaspoon salt

¼ cup chicken broth

1 teaspoon dried cilantro

Method

1.   Put all ingredients in the instant pot and stir until you get the red color of the cauliflower.

2.   Close and seal the lid.

3.   Cook the meal on manual (high pressure) for 3 minutes. Make a quick pressure release.

Nutritional info per serve: calories 79, fat 7.3, fiber 1.3, carbs 3.3, protein 1.6

Steamed Spinach with Garlic

Prep time: 5 minutes | **Cook time:** 4 minutes | **Yield:** 4 servings

Ingredients

2 cups spinach, chopped

1 cup organic almond milk

1 teaspoon minced garlic

1 tablespoon butter

½ teaspoon salt

2 oz Monterey Jack cheese, shredded

Method

1.   Put all ingredients in the instant pot and stir gently.

2.   Close and seal the lid.

3.   Cook the meal on manual mode (high pressure) for 4 minutes. Make a quick pressure release.

4.   After this, open the lid and stir the spinach well.

Nutritional info per serve: calories 98, fat 7.9, fiber 0.3, carbs 2.9, protein 4.2

Lemon Mushrooms

Prep time: 10 minutes | **Cook time:** 4 minutes | **Yield:** 2 servings

Ingredients

1 cup cremini mushrooms, sliced

1 teaspoon lemon zest, grated

1 tablespoon lemon juice

½ teaspoon salt

½ teaspoon dried thyme

½ cup of water

1 teaspoon almond butter

Method

1.   Put all ingredients in the instant pot and stir them with the help of the spatula.

2.   Then close and seal the instant pot lid.

3.   Cook the mushrooms on manual mode (high pressure) for 4 minutes.

4.   When the time of cooking is finished, allow the natural pressure release for 5 minutes.

Nutritional info per serve: calories 62, fat 4.6, fiber 1.2, carbs 3.5, protein 2.7

Feta Psiti

Prep time: 10 minutes | **Cook time:** 6 minutes | **Yield:** 6 servings

Ingredients

12 oz Feta cheese

½ tomato, sliced

1 oz bell pepper, sliced

1 teaspoon ground paprika

1 tablespoon olive oil

1 cup water, for cooking

Method

1.   Sprinkle the cheese with olive oil and ground paprika and place it on the foil.

2.   Then top Feta cheese with sliced tomato and bell pepper. Wrap it in the foil well.

3.   After this, pour water and insert the steamer rack in the instant pot.

4.   Put the wrapped cheese on the rack. Close and seal the lid.

5.   Cook the cheese on manual mode (high pressure) for 6 minutes. Then make a quick pressure release.

6.   Discard the foil and transfer the cheese on the serving plates.

Nutritional info per serve: calories 178, fat 14.5, fiber 0.5, carbs 4.2, protein 8.4

Steamed Savoy Cabbage

Prep time: 5 minutes | **Cook time:** 7 minutes | **Yield:** 4 servings

Ingredients

1-pound savoy cabbage, chopped

1/3 cup butter

1 teaspoon salt

½ teaspoon white pepper

1 cup chicken broth

Method

1.   Put all ingredients in the instant pot and stir them well.

2.   After this, close and seal the lid.

3.   Cook the savoy cabbage on manual mode (high pressure) for 7 minutes.

4.   Then make a quick pressure release and open the lid.

5.   Stir the meal well before serving.

Nutritional info per serve: calories 174, fat 15.8, fiber 2.9, carbs 7, protein 2.9

Sesame Broccoli Sprouts

Prep time: 5 minutes | **Cook time:** 1 minute |
Yield: 4 servings

Ingredients

1-pound broccoli sprouts

1 cup of water

1 teaspoon coconut aminos

½ teaspoon chili pepper, chopped

½ teaspoon salt

1 teaspoon minced garlic

1 teaspoon sesame oil

Method

1.   Pour water in the instant pot. Close the lid.

2.   Bring the water to boil on saute mode (appx. 10 minutes).

3.   Then open the lid and add broccoli sprouts. Leave the sprouts in the hot water for 1 minute.

4.   Then transfer the sprouts in the bowl.

5.   In the separated bowl, mix up coconut aminos, chili pepper, salt, minced garlic, and sesame oil.

6.   Pour mixture over the broccoli sprouts. Shake the greens.

Nutritional info per serve: calories 53, fat 1.1, fiber 4, carbs 4.6, protein 4.1

Faux-Tatoes

Prep time: 5 minutes | **Cook time:** 18 minutes |
Yield: 4 servings

Ingredients

1 daikon radish, sliced

3 oz scallions, diced

1 tablespoon coconut oil

1 teaspoon salt

Method

1.   Mix up daikon radish and scallions in the bowl and sprinkle with salt.

2.   Then toss the coconut oil in the instant pot and melt it on saute mode.

3.   Add daikon radish mixture and close the lid.

4.   Saute the vegetables for 5 minutes and turn into another side.

5.   Cook the vegetables for 10 minutes more. Stir them from time to time.

Nutritional info per serve: calories 39, fat 3.4, fiber 0.8, carbs 2.1, protein 0.6

Steamed Kohlrabi

Prep time: 5 minutes | **Cook time:** 8 minutes |
Yield: 5 servings

Ingredients

14 oz kohlrabi, chopped

½ garlic clove, diced

1 tablespoon avocado oil

½ teaspoon salt

½ cup chicken broth

Method

1.   Pour avocado oil in the instant pot and add diced garlic.

2.   Saute the ingredients for 3 minutes.

3.   Add chopped kohlrabi and cook the greens for 2 minutes more.

4.   After this, sprinkle them with salt and add chicken broth.

5.   Close and seal the lid and cook the meal on the "steam" mode for 3 minutes.

6.   Make a quick pressure release.

Nutritional info per serve: calories 29, fat 0.6, fiber 3, carbs 5.3, protein 1.9

Broccoli Skewers

Prep time: 15 minutes | **Cook time:** 1 minute |
Yield: 2 servings

Ingredients

1 cup broccoli florets

½ teaspoon curry paste

2 tablespoons coconut cream

1 cup water, for cooking

Method

1.   In the shallow bowl mix up curry paste and coconut cream.

2.   Then sprinkle the broccoli florets with curry paste mixture and string on the skewers.

3.   Pour water and insert the steamer rack in the instant pot.

4.   Place the broccoli skewers on the rack. Close and seal the lid.

5.   Cook the meal on manual mode (high pressure) for 1 minute.

6.   Make a quick pressure release.

Nutritional info per serve: calories 58, fat 4.5, fiber 1.5, carbs 4.2, protein 1.7

Garlic Shirataki Noodles

Prep time: 10 minutes | **Cook time:** 3 minutes |
Yield: 4 servings

Ingredients

7 oz shirataki noodles

1 garlic clove, minced

1 tablespoon olive oil

1 teaspoon fresh cilantro, chopped

1 cup hot water

Method

1.   Put shirataki noodles in the hot water and leave them for 3 minutes.

2.   Meanwhile, pour olive oil in the instant pot.

3.   Add minced garlic and saute it for 2 minutes.

4.   Stir well.

5.   After this, remove the noodles from water and transfer in the instant pot.

6.   Add chopped cilantro and stir well. Cook the meal for 1 minute more.

Nutritional info per serve: calories 42, fat 3.5, fiber 5.3, carbs 0.3, protein 0.4

Steamed Fennel Bulb

Prep time: 10 minutes | **Cook time:** 7 minutes |
Yield: 2 servings

Ingredients

8 oz fennel bulb, chopped

1 teaspoon olive oil

1 teaspoon

¼ teaspoon cayenne pepper

¼ teaspoon

1 cup water, for cooking

Method

1.   Pour water and insert the steamer rack in the instant pot.

2.   Place the chopped fennel in the steamer rack. Close and seal the lid.

3.   Cook the vegetables on steam mode for 7 minutes. Make a quick pressure release.

4.   After this, transfer the fennel in the bog bowl and sprinkle with olive oil, coconut aminos, cayenne pepper, and Splenda.

5.   Mix up the vegetables well.

Nutritional info per serve: calories 61, fat 2.6, fiber 3.6, carbs 9.4, protein 1.4

Shrimp Sandwich

Prep time: 5 minutes | **Cook time:** 5 minutes | **Yield:** 2 servings

Ingredients

4 lettuce leaves

4 king shrimps, peeled

1 teaspoon lemon juice

½ teaspoon white pepper

2 tablespoons butter

½ teaspoon salt

Method

1.   Sprinkle the shrimps with white pepper and salt and put in the instant pot.

2.   Add butter and cook the seafood for 3 minutes on saute mode.

3.   Then flip the shrimps on another side and cook them for 2 minutes more.

4.   Sprinkle the cooked shrimps with lemon juice and transfer on lettuce leaves (2 shrimps per one lettuce leaf).

5.   Cover them with the remaining lettuce.

Nutritional info per serve: calories 165, fat 12.6, fiber 0.2, carbs 0.7, protein 12.3

SOUP AND STEWS

Broccoli Cheese Soup

Prep time: 10 minutes | **Cook time:** 5 minutes | **Yield:** 4 servings

Ingredients

2 cups broccoli florets

1 cup Cheddar cheese, shredded

2 garlic cloves, diced

1 tablespoon olive oil

1 cup heavy cream

2 cups chicken broth

½ teaspoon ground black pepper

Method

1. Heat up olive oil in the instant pot.
2. Then add diced garlic and saute it for 2 minutes.
3. After this, add broccoli florets, shredded cheese, heavy cream, and chicken broth.
4. Add ground black pepper and close the lid.
5. Cook the soup on manual mode (High pressure) for 3 minutes.
6. Then allow the natural pressure release for 5 minutes.

Nutritional info per serve: calories 285, fat 24.8, fiber 1.3, carbs 5.4, protein 11.5

Gumbo

Prep time: 10 minutes | **Cook time:** 15 minutes | **Yield:** 4 servings

Ingredients

2 chicken thighs, boneless, chopped

4 oz shrimps, peeled

½ bell pepper, chopped

3 oz sausages, chopped

1 celery stalk, chopped

1 cup beef broth

1 teaspoon tomato paste

½ teaspoon Cajun seasonings

Method

1. Heat up the instant pot on saute mode for 3 minutes.
2. Then add chicken thighs, shrimps, bell pepper, sausages, celery stalk, beef broth, tomato paste, and Cajun seasonings.
3. Gently mix up the ingredients and close the lid.
4. Cook the gumbo for 15 minutes on manual mode (high pressure).
5. Then make a quick pressure release and stir the meal well.

Nutritional info per serve: calories 261, fat 12.3, fiber 0.3, carbs 2.2, protein 33.2

Chicken Soup

Prep time: 10 minutes | **Cook time:** 20 minutes | **Yield:** 2 servings

Ingredients

8 oz chicken breast, skinless, boneless

2 cups of water

1 tablespoon scallions, diced

1 teaspoon salt

1 tablespoon fresh dill, chopped

Method

1. Pour water in the instant pot.
2. Chop the chicken breast and add it in the water.
3. Then add scallions, salt, and close the lid.
4. Cook the soup on manual mode (high pressure) for 20 minutes.
5. Then make a quick pressure release and ladle the soup in the bowls.
6. Top the soup with fresh dill.

Nutritional info per serve: calories 134, fat 2.9, fiber 0.3, carbs 1.1, protein 24.4

Taco Soup

Prep time: 15 minutes | **Cook time:** 20 minutes | **Yield:** 6 servings

Ingredients

1 cup ground beef
1 bell pepper, chopped
1 garlic clove, diced
½ cup crushed tomatoes
2 tablespoons cream cheese
4 cups beef broth
1 tablespoon coconut oil
1 teaspoon taco seasonings

Method

1. Heat up coconut oil in the instant pot on saute mode.
2. Then add ground beef and sprinkle it with taco seasonings. Stir well and cook the meat on saute mode for 5 minutes.
3. After this, add bell pepper, garlic clove, crushed tomatoes, cream cheese, and beef broth.

4. Close the lid and cook the soup on manual mode (high pressure) for 15 minutes.
5. Then allow the natural pressure release for 10 minutes and open the lid.
6. Ladle the soup.

Nutritional info per serve: calories 117, fat 7.1, fiber 1, carbs 4.4, protein 8.6

Tuscan Soup

Prep time: 15 minutes | **Cook time:** 13 minutes | **Yield:** 3 servings

Ingredients

1 bacon slice, chopped
2 oz scallions, diced
½ teaspoon garlic powder
6 oz Italian sausages, chopped
¼ cup cauliflower, chopped
3 cups chicken broth
1 cup kale, chopped
¼ cup heavy cream

Method

1. Heat up the instant pot on saute mode for 3 minutes.
2. Then add chopped bacon and cook it for 2 minutes on saute mode.
3. Stir it well and add scallions.
4. Add garlic powder, Italian sausages, and cauliflower.
5. Mix up the ingredients and cook them for 5 minutes on saute mode.
6. After this, add chicken broth, kale, and heavy cream.
7. Cook the soup on manual mode (high pressure) for 6 minutes. Then make a quick pressure release.

Nutritional info per serve: calories 324, fat 25.5, fiber 1.1, carbs 6.7, protein 16.7

Cheeseburger Soup

Prep time: 10 minutes | **Cook time:** 11 minutes | **Yield:** 5 servings

Ingredients

1 cup ground pork

1 teaspoon mustard powder

4 cups beef broth

1 teaspoon cayenne pepper

1 teaspoon coconut oil

½ cup Monterey jack cheese, shredded

2 tablespoons cream cheese

3 tablespoons heavy cream

Method

1.   In the mixing bowl, mix up ground pork, mustard powder, and cayenne pepper.

2.   Then melt the coconut oil in the instant pot on saute mode.

3.   Add the ground pork mixture and saute it for 6 minutes.

4.   Then stir the mixture well and add cream cheese and heavy cream. Add beef broth and close the lid.

5.   Cook the soup on manual mode (high pressure) for 5 minutes.

6.   Then make a quick pressure release and ladle the soup in the bowls.

7.   Top the soup with Monterey Jack cheese.

Nutritional info per serve: calories 316, fat 23.4, fiber 0.2, carbs 1.6, protein 23.4

Cabbage Soup

Prep time: 10 minutes | **Cook time:** 12 minutes | **Yield:** 3 servings

Ingredients

½ cup ground pork

½ cup white cabbage, shredded

2 cups chicken broth

½ teaspoon ground coriander

½ teaspoon salt

1 teaspoon butter

½ teaspoon chili flakes

Method

1.   Melt the butter in the instant pot on saute mode.

2.   Add cabbage and sprinkle it with ground coriander, salt, and chili flakes.

3.   Add chicken broth and ground pork.

4.   Close and seal the lid and cook the soup on manual mode (high pressure) for 12 minutes.

Nutritional info per serve: calories 350, fat 23.9, fiber 0.3, carbs 1.3, protein 30.2

Cauliflower Soup

Prep time: 15 minutes | **Cook time:** 6 minutes | **Yield:** 4 servings

Ingredients

2 cups cauliflower, chopped

1 cup coconut cream

2 cups beef broth

2 tablespoons fresh cilantro

3 oz Provolone cheese, chopped

Method

1.   Put cauliflower, coconut cream, beef broth, cilantro, and cheese in the instant pot.

2. Cook the soup on manual (high pressure) for 6 minutes. Then allow the natural pressure release for 4 minutes.

3. Blend the soup with the help of the immersion blender.

Nutritional info per serve: calories 244, fat 20.7, fiber 2.6, carbs 6.9, protein 10.2

Beef Stew

Prep time: 10 minutes | **Cook time:** 30 minutes | **Yield:** 4 servings

Ingredients

½ cup Brussel sprouts

4 cups of water

1 teaspoon tomato paste

12 oz beef sirloin, chopped

1 tablespoon sesame oil

½ teaspoon salt

1 bay leaf

½ teaspoon peppercorns

Method

1. Put all ingredients in the instant pot and close the lid.

2. Cook the stew on Manual mode (high pressure) for 30 minutes.

3. The cooked stew should have a very tender structure.

Nutritional info per serve: calories 195, fat 8.8, fiber 0.6, carbs 1.6, protein 26.3

Curry Stew with Chicken

Prep time: 10 minutes | **Cook time:** 12 minutes | **Yield:** 4 servings

Ingredients

1 teaspoon curry paste

1 teaspoon grated lemon zest

4 oz leek, chopped

2 cups of water

1 tablespoon coconut cream

4 chicken thighs, skinless, boneless, chopped

Method

1. In the mixing bowl, mix up coconut cream, grated lemon zest, and curry paste.

2. Then mix up chopped chicken thighs and curry paste mixture.

3. Put the mixture in the instant pot and add leek and water.

4. Close the lid and cook the stew for 12 minutes on manual mode (high pressure).

5. Then make a quick pressure release and transfer the stew in the plates/bowls.

Nutritional info per serve: calories 145, fat 4.6, fiber 0.6, carbs 4.7, protein 20.4

Chicken Paprikash

Prep time: 10 minutes | **Cook time:** 18 minutes | **Yield:** 4 servings

Ingredients

1 tablespoon ground paprika

¼ cup scallions, diced

1 bell pepper, chopped

4 chicken thighs, skinless

1 teaspoon coconut oil

½ teaspoon salt

½ teaspoon ground cumin

4 cups chicken broth

Method

1.   Heat up coconut oil in the instant pot on Saute mode.

2.   When the oil is melted. Add chicken thighs and cook them for 4 minutes from each side.

3.   After this, sprinkle the chicken scallions, bell pepper, salt, and ground cumin. Gently mix up the ingredients. Add paprika.

4.   Add chicken broth and close the lid.

5.   Cook the paprikash for 10 minutes on Manual mode (high pressure). Then make a quick pressure release.

Nutritional info per serve: calories 343, fat 13.7, fiber 1.2, carbs 4.7, protein 47.8

Pork Stew

Prep time: 15 minutes | **Cook time:** 3 minutes | **Yield:** 6 servings

Ingredients

½ cup daikon, chopped

1 oz green onions, chopped

1-pound pork tenderloin, chopped

1 lemon slice

1 teaspoon ground black pepper

1 tablespoon butter

1 tablespoon heavy cream

3 cups of water

Method

1.   Put all ingredients in the instant pot and mix up them with the help of the spatula.

2.   Then close and seal the lid. Set manual mode (high pressure) and cook the stew for 20 minutes.

3.   Allow the natural pressure release for 15 minutes.

Nutritional info per serve: calories 137, fat 5.5, fiber 0.3, carbs 0.9, protein 20.1

Italian Style Lamb Stew

Prep time: 10 minutes | **Cook time:** 52 minutes | **Yield:** 5 servings

Ingredients

1-pound lamb shank, chopped

1 teaspoon dried rosemary

1 turnip, chopped

½ teaspoon salt

1 teaspoon tomato paste

1 teaspoon olive oil

2 cups of water

Method

1.   Heat up olive oil on saute mode for 2 minutes.

2.   Then add turnip, chopped lamb shank, and dried rosemary. Saute the ingredients for 5 minutes.

3.   After this, add water and tomato paste. Close the lid and cook the stew on saute mode for 45 minutes.

Nutritional info per serve: calories 185, fat 7.7, fiber 0.6, carbs 1.9, protein 25.8

Cheesy Cream Soup

Prep time: 15 minutes | **Cook time:** 20 minutes | **Yield:** 4 servings

Ingredients

3 tablespoons cream cheese

2 oz blue cheese, crumbled

2 cups white mushrooms, chopped

4 oz scallions, diced

4 cups chicken broth

1 teaspoon salt

1 teaspoon olive oil

½ teaspoon ground cumin

Method

1.   Put cream cheese, mushrooms, scallions, chicken broth, olive oil, and ground cumin in the instant pot.

2.   Close and seal the lid.

3.   Cook the soup mixture for 20 minutes on manual mode (high pressure).

4.   Then make a quick pressure release and open the lid.

5.   Add salt and blend the soup with the help of the immersion blender.

6.   Then ladle the soup in the bowls and top with blue cheese.

Nutritional info per serve: calories 142, fat 9.4, fiber 1.1, carbs 4.8, protein 10.1

Seafood Stew

Prep time: 10 minutes | **Cook time:** 20 minutes | **Yield:** 4 servings

Ingredients

½ teaspoon ground cumin

½ teaspoon ground paprika

½ teaspoon ground turmeric

8 oz cod, chopped

½ cup crushed tomatoes

1 teaspoon coconut oil

½ teaspoon sesame seeds

Method

1.   Sprinkle the chopped cod with cumin, paprika, turmeric, and sesame seeds.

2.   Then heat up coconut oil in the instant pot on saute mode.

3.   Add cod and cook it for 2 minutes from each side.

4.   Then add crushed tomatoes and close the lid.

5.   Saute the stew for 15 minutes.

Nutritional info per serve: calories 87, fat 1.9, fiber 1.2, carbs 3, protein 13.9

Okra and Beef Stew

Prep time: 15 minutes | **Cook time:** 25 minutes | **Yield:** 3 servings

Ingredients

6 oz okra, chopped

8 oz beef sirloin, chopped

1 cup of water

¼ cup coconut cream

1 teaspoon dried basil

¼ teaspoon cumin seeds

1 tablespoon avocado oil

Method

1.   Sprinkle the beef sirloin with cumin seeds and dried basil and put in the instant pot.

2. Add avocado oil and roast the meat on saute mode for 5 minutes. Stir it occasionally.

3. Then add coconut cream, water, and okra.

4. Close the lid and cook the stew on manual mode (high pressure) for 25 minutes. Allow the natural pressure release for 10 minutes.

Nutritional info per serve: calories 216, fat 10.2, fiber 2.5, carbs 5.7, protein 24.6

Chipotle Stew

Prep time: 15 minutes | **Cook time:** 10 minutes | **Yield:** 3 servings

Ingredients

2 chipotle chili in adobo sauce, chopped

1 oz fresh cilantro, chopped

9 oz chicken fillet, chopped

1 teaspoon ground paprika

2 tablespoons sesame seeds

¼ teaspoon salt

1 cup chicken broth

Method

1. In the mixing bowl mix up chipotle chili, cilantro, chicken fillet, ground paprika, sesame seeds, and salt.

2. Then transfer the ingredients in the instant pot and add chicken broth.

3. Cook the stew on manual mode (high pressure) for 10 minutes. Allow the natural pressure release for 10 minutes more.

Nutritional info per serve: calories 230, fat 10.6, fiber 2.6, carbs 4.5, protein 27.6

Keto Chili

Prep time: 10 minutes | **Cook time:** 25 minutes | **Yield:** 2 servings

Ingredients

½ cup ground beef

½ teaspoon chili powder

1 teaspoon dried oregano

¼ cup crushed tomatoes

2 oz scallions, diced

1 teaspoon avocado oil

¼ cup of water

Method

1. Mix up ground beef, chili powder, dried oregano, and scallions.

2. Then add avocado oil and stir the mixture.

3. Transfer it in the instant pot and cook on saute mode for 10 minutes.

4. Add water and crushed tomatoes. Stir the ingredients with the help of the spatula until homogenous.

5. Close and seal the lid and cook the chili for 15 minutes on manual mode (high pressure). Then make a quick pressure release.

Nutritional info per serve: calories 94, fat 4.6, fiber 2.4, carbs 5.6, protein 8

Pizza Soup

Prep time: 10 minutes | **Cook time:** 22 minutes | **Yield:** 3 servings

Ingredients

¼ cup cremini mushrooms, sliced

1 teaspoon tomato paste

4 oz Mozzarella, shredded

½ jalapeno pepper, sliced

½ teaspoon Italian seasoning

1 teaspoon coconut oil

5 oz Italian sausages, chopped

1 cup of water

Method

1.   Melt the coconut oil in the instant pot on saute mode.

2.   Add mushrooms and cook them for 10 minutes.

3.   After this, add chopped sausages, Italian seasoning, sliced jalapeno, and tomato paste.

4.   Mix up the ingredients well and add water.

5.   Close and seal the lid and cook the soup on manual mode (high pressure) for 12 minutes.

6.   Then make a quick pressure release and ladle the soup in the bowls. Top it with Mozzarella.

Nutritional info per serve: calories 289, fat 23.2, fiber 0.2, carbs 2.5, protein 17.7

Lamb Soup

Prep time: 10 minutes | **Cook time:** 25 minutes | **Yield:** 4 servings

Ingredients

½ cup broccoli, roughly chopped

7 oz lamb fillet, chopped

¼ teaspoon ground cumin

¼ daikon, chopped

2 bell peppers, chopped

1 tablespoon avocado oil

5 cups beef broth

Method

1.   Saute the lamb fillet with avocado oil in the instant pot for 5 minutes.

2.   Then add broccoli, ground cumin, daikon, bell peppers, and beef broth.

3.   Close and seal the lid.

4.   Cook the soup on manual mode (high pressure) for 20 minutes.

5.   Allow the natural pressure release.

Nutritional info per serve: calories 169, fat 6, fiber 1.3, carbs 6.8, protein 21

Minestrone Soup

Prep time: 10 minutes | **Cook time:** 25 minutes | **Yield:** 4 servings

Ingredients

1 ½ cup ground pork

½ bell pepper, chopped

2 tablespoons chives, chopped

2 oz celery stalk, chopped

1 teaspoon butter

1 teaspoon Italian seasonings

4 cups chicken broth

½ cup mushrooms, sliced

Method

1.   Heat up butter on the saute mode for 2 minutes.

2.   Add bell pepper. Cook the vegetable for 5 minutes.

3.   Then stir them well and add mushrooms, celery stalk, and Italian seasonings. Stir well and cook for 5 minutes more.

4.   Add ground pork, chives, and chicken broth.

5.   Close and seal the lid.

6. Cook the soup on manual mode (high pressure) for 15 minutes. Make a quick pressure release.

Nutritional info per serve: calories 408, fat 27.2, fiber 0.6, carbs 3, protein 35.6

Chorizo Soup

Prep time: 10 minutes | **Cook time:** 17 minutes | **Yield:** 3 servings

Ingredients

8 oz chorizo, chopped

1 teaspoon tomato paste

4 oz scallions, diced

1 tablespoon dried cilantro

½ teaspoon chili powder

1 teaspoon avocado oil

2 cups beef broth

Method

1. Heat up avocado oil on saute mode for 1 minute.

2. Add chorizo and cook it for 6 minutes, stir it from time to time.

3. Then add scallions, tomato paste, cilantro, and chili powder. Stir well.

4. Add beef broth.

5. Close and seal the lid.

6. Cook the soup on manual mode (high pressure) for 10 minutes. Make a quick pressure release.

Nutritional info per serve: calories 387, fat 30.2, fiber 1.3, carbs 5.5, protein 22.3

Red Feta Soup

Prep time: 10 minutes | **Cook time:** 25 minutes | **Yield:** 4 servings

Ingredients

1 cup broccoli, chopped

1 teaspoon tomato paste

½ cup coconut cream

4 cups beef broth

1 teaspoon chili flakes

6 oz feta, crumbled

Method

1. Put broccoli, tomato paste, coconut cream, and beef broth in the instant pot.

2. Add chili flakes and stir the mixture until it is red.

3. Then close and seal the lid and cook the soup for 8 minutes on manual mode (high pressure).

4. Then make a quick pressure release and open the lid.

5. Add feta cheese and saute the soup on saute mode for 5 minutes more.

Nutritional info per serve: calories 229, fat 17.7, fiber 1.3, carbs 6.1, protein 12.3

"Ramen" Soup

Prep time: 10 minutes | **Cook time:** 15 minutes | **Yield:** 2 servings

Ingredients

1 zucchini, trimmed

2 cups chicken broth

2 eggs, boiled, peeled

1 tablespoon coconut aminos

5 oz beef loin, strips

1 teaspoon chili flakes

1 tablespoon chives, chopped

½ teaspoon salt

Method

1. Put the beef loin strips in the instant pot.

2. Add chili flakes, salt, and chicken broth.

3. Close and seal the lid. Cook the ingredients on manual mode (high pressure) for 15 minutes. Make a quick pressure release and open the lid.

4. Then make the s from zucchini with the help of the spiralizer and add them in the soup.

5. Add chives and coconut aminos.

6. Then ladle the soup in the bowls and top with halved eggs.

Nutritional info per serve: calories 254, fat 11.8, fiber 1.1, carbs 6.2, protein 30.6

Beef Tagine

Prep time: 15 minutes | **Cook time:** 25 minutes | **Yield:** 6 servings

Ingredients

1-pound beef fillet, chopped

1 eggplant, chopped

6 oz scallions, chopped

1 teaspoon ground allspices

1 teaspoon Erythritol

1 teaspoon coconut oil

4 cups beef broth

Method

1. Put all ingredients in the instant pot.

2. Close and seal the lid.

3. Cook the meal on manual mode (high pressure) for 25 minutes.

4. Then allow the natural pressure release for 15 minutes.

Nutritional info per serve: calories 146, fat 5.3, fiber 3.5, carbs 8.8, protein 16.7

BEEF AND LAMB

Beef Pot Roast

Prep time: 20 minutes | **Cook time:** 40 minutes | **Yield:** 5 servings

Ingredients

1-pound beef chuck roast, chopped

1 teaspoon salt

4 tablespoon apple cider vinegar

¾ teaspoon xanthan gum

1 cup beef broth

1 teaspoon olive oil

Method

1.   Sprinkle the beef with olive oil and salt.

2.   Then put it in the instant pot and add beef broth, apple cider vinegar, and xanthan gum. Stir the ingredients gently with the help of the spoon. Close and seal the lid.

3.   Cook the meal on manual mode (high pressure) for 40 minutes.

4.   Then allow the natural pressure release for 10 minutes.

Nutritional info per serve: calories 350, fat 26.4, fiber 0.7, carbs 1, protein 24.7

Mongolian Beef

Prep time: 10 minutes | **Cook time:** 45 minutes | **Yield:** 4 servings

Ingredients

1 tablespoon coconut aminos

¼ teaspoon garlic, minced

1 teaspoon Erythritol

1 teaspoon sesame oil

¼ teaspoon ground ginger

1-pound flank steak

¼ cup of water

Method

1.   In the mixing bowl mix up coconut aminos, minced garlic, Erythritol, and ground ginger.

2.   Slice the flank steak and mix it up with coconut aminos mixture.

3.   Heat up sesame oil on saute mode for 1 minute and add sliced flank steal

4.   Cook it for 10 minutes on saute mode. Stir it from time to time.

5.   Then add water and close the lid.

6.   Cook the beef on saute mode for 35 minutes.

Nutritional info per serve: calories 234, fat 10.6, fiber 0, carbs 0.9, protein 31.6

Thyme Beef Brisket

Prep time: 10 minutes | **Cook time:** 25 minutes | **Yield:** 3 servings

Ingredients

1 teaspoon dried thyme

12 oz beef brisket, chopped

½ cup of water

½ teaspoon salt

1 teaspoon coconut oil

Method

1.   Sprinkle the beef brisket with salt and dried thyme.

2. Then melt the coconut oil in the instant pot on saute mode and add beef brisket.

3. Add water and close the lid.

4. Cook the meat on manual mode (high pressure) for 25 minutes.

5. Then allow the natural pressure release for 10 minutes.

Nutritional info per serve: calories 225, fat 8.6, fiber 0.1, carbs 0.2, protein 34.4

Goulash

Prep time: 10 minutes | **Cook time:** 35 minutes | **Yield:** 4 servings

Ingredients

1-pound beef sirloin, chopped

1 bell pepper, chopped

2 celery stalks, chopped

1 teaspoon coconut oil

1 teaspoon chili flakes

1 cup of water

Method

1. Put the coconut oil and chopped beef sirloin in the instant pot.

2. Cook it on sauté mode for 5 minutes. Stir it with the help of a spatula and add chili flakes.

3. Then add celery stalk and water.

4. Add bell pepper. Close and seal the lid.

5. Cook the goulash for 30 minutes on manual mode (high pressure). Make a quick pressure release.

Nutritional info per serve: calories 231, fat 8.3, fiber 0.6, carbs 2.5, protein 34.8

Beef Pot Round Steak

Prep time: 10 minutes | **Cook time:** 25 minutes | **Yield:** 2 servings

Ingredients

2 pork round steaks

2 tablespoons avocado oil

1 teaspoon white pepper

½ teaspoon salt

1 teaspoon cayenne pepper

1 cup of water

Method

1. Rub the round steaks with avocado oil, white pepper, salt, and cayenne pepper.

2. Then wrap it in the foil.

3. Pour water and insert the rack in the instant pot.

4. Then put the wrapped steaks on the rack. Close and seal the lid.

5. Cook the steaks on manual mode (high pressure) for 25 minutes.

6. When the time is over, make a quick pressure release and open the lid.

7. Remove the steaks from the foil.

Nutritional info per serve: calories 334, fat 21, fiber 2.1, carbs 8, protein 29.4

Steak Bites

Prep time: 10 minutes | **Cook time:** 35 minutes | **Yield:** 6 servings

Ingredients

1-pound beef sirloin steak

3 tablespoons coconut aminos

1 teaspoon red pepper flakes

½ teaspoon minced garlic

3 tablespoons sesame oil

Method

1.   Cut the beef sirloin steak on small cubes (bites) and sprinkle them with coconut aminos, red pepper flakes, minced garlic, and sesame oil.

2.   Leave the meat for 10 minutes to marinate.

3.   Then heat up the instant pot on saute mode.

4.   Add the beef bites and close the lid.

5.   Cook the meal for 35 minutes on saute mode. Stir it every 5 minutes to avoid burning.

Nutritional info per serve: calories 209, fat 11.6, fiber 0.1, carbs 1.8, protein 23

Hibachi Steak

Prep time: 10 minutes | **Cook time:** 10 minutes | **Yield:** 4 servings

Ingredients

1-pound beef sirloin, roughly chopped

1 teaspoon ground ginger

¼ teaspoon garlic powder

¼ cup cremini mushrooms, sliced

2 tablespoons apple cider vinegar

1 tablespoon avocado oil

¼ cup of water

Method

1.   Mix up beef sirloin, ground ginger, garlic powder, apple cider vinegar, mushrooms, and avocado oil.

2.   Transfer the ingredients in the instant pot. Add water.

3.   Close and seal the lid and cook the meal on manual mode (high pressure) for 10 minutes. Allow the natural pressure release for 10 minutes.

Nutritional info per serve: calories 220, fat 7.5, fiber 0.3, carbs 0.9, protein 34.6

Beef Burgundy

Prep time: 15 minutes | **Cook time:** 35 minutes | **Yield:** 6 servings

Ingredients

3 oz bacon, chopped

1-pound beef tenderloin, chopped

1 teaspoon tomato paste

¼ cup apple cider vinegar

1 cup beef broth

¼ teaspoon xanthan gum

¼ teaspoon ground coriander

1 teaspoon dried oregano

Method

1.   Put the bacon in the instant pot and cook it for 5 minutes on saute mode.

2.   Stir the bacon with the help of the spatula every 1 minute.

3.   Then add chopped beef tenderloin, apple cider vinegar, xanthan gum, ground coriander, and dried oregano.

4.   Then add tomato paste and mix up the meat mixture.

5.   Add beef broth and close the lid.

6.   Cook the meal on manual mode (high pressure) for 30 minutes. Make a quick pressure release.

Nutritional info per serve: calories 245, fat 13.1, fiber 0.7, carbs 1.3, protein 28

Beef Gyros Stuffing

Prep time: 10 minutes | **Cook time:** 22 minutes | **Yield:** 2 servings

Ingredients

5 oz beef chuck, sliced

1 teaspoon chives, chopped

¾ cup beef broth

1 teaspoon coconut aminos

½ teaspoon olive oil

¼ teaspoon Italian seasonings

Method

1.   Put the sliced beef chuck in the instant pot.

2.   Add chives, beef broth, coconut aminos, olive oil, and Italian seasonings.

3.   Cook the beef gyros stuffing for 22 minutes on saute mode. Mix it up every 5 minutes.

Nutritional info per serve: calories 160, fat 6.3, fiber 0, carbs 0.9, protein 23.3

Butter Beef

Prep time: 10 minutes | **Cook time:** 7 hours | **Yield:** 4 servings

Ingredients

1-pound beef steak

½ cup butter, softened

1 teaspoon ground nutmeg

½ teaspoon salt

Method

1.   Heat up butter in the instant pot on saute mode.

2.   When the butter is melted, add beef steak, ground nutmeg, and salt.

3.   Close the lid and cook the meat on slow cook mode for 7 hours.

Nutritional info per serve: calories 417, fat 30.3, fiber 0.1, carbs 0.3, protein 34.7

Lamb Shank with Spices

Prep time: 15 minutes | **Cook time:** 35 minutes | **Yield:** 2 servings

Ingredients

2 lamb shanks

¼ teaspoon chili powder

1 rosemary spring

1 teaspoon coconut flour

¼ teaspoon onion powder

¾ teaspoon ground ginger

½ cup beef broth

½ teaspoon avocado oil

Method

1.   Put all ingredients in the instant pot.

2.   Close and seal the lid.

3.   Cook the meat on manual mode (high pressure) for 35 minutes.

4.   Then allow the natural pressure release for 15 minutes.

Nutritional info per serve: calories 179, fat 7, fiber 0.8, carbs 2, protein 25.4

Greek Style Leg of Lamb

Prep time: 10 minutes | **Cook time:** 50 minutes | **Yield:** 4 servings

Ingredients

1-pound leg of lamb

2 garlic cloves, peeled

1 teaspoon paprika powder

½ teaspoon dried thyme

¼ teaspoon cumin seeds

¼ cup of water

1 tablespoon butter

Method

1.   Rub the leg of lamb with paprika powder, dried thyme, and cumin seeds.

2.   Then gently brush it with softened butter and transfer in the instant pot.

3.   Add garlic cloves and water.

4.   Close and seal the lid.

5.   Cook the meal on manual mode (high pressure) for 50 minutes. Make a quick pressure release.

Nutritional info per serve: calories 239, fat 11.2, fiber 0.1, carbs 0.6, protein 32

Lamb Curry

Prep time: 10 minutes | **Cook time:** 30 minutes | **Yield:** 4 servings

Ingredients

1-pound lamb shoulder, chopped

1 teaspoon curry paste

2 tablespoons coconut cream

¼ teaspoon chili powder

1 tablespoon fresh cilantro, chopped

½ cup heavy cream

Method

1.   In the shallow bowl mix up curry paste and coconut cream.

2.   Add chili powder and chopped lamb shoulder. Coat the meat in the curry mixture well.

3.   Then transfer the meat and all remaining curry paste mixture in the instant pot.

4.   Add cilantro and heavy cream.

5.   Close and seal the lid and cook the meal for 30 minutes on manual mode (high pressure). Make a quick pressure release.

Nutritional info per serve: calories 289, fat 16.4, fiber 0.2, carbs 1.3, protein 32.4

Persian Lamb

Prep time: 10 minutes | **Cook time:** 40 minutes | **Yield:** 4 servings

Ingredients

¼ cup pomegranate juice

¼ teaspoon ground coriander

1 oz scallions, chopped

1-pound lamb fillet, chopped

1 teaspoon coconut oil

½ cup of water

Method

1.   Heat up the coconut oil on saute mode for 2 minutes.

2.   Add lamb fillet and cook it on saute mode for 5 minutes.

3.   Then stir it well and add scallions, ground coriander, and pomegranate juice.

4.   Add water, close and seal the lid.

5.   Cook the meat for 32 minutes on manual mode (high pressure). Make a quick pressure release.

Nutritional info per serve: calories 232, fat 9.5, fiber 0.2, carbs 2.8, protein 32

Lamb Roast

Prep time: 10 minutes | **Cook time:** 25 minutes | **Yield:** 3 servings

Ingredients

14 oz leg of lamb, roughly chopped

1 teaspoon ground black pepper

1 teaspoon dried thyme

1 tablespoon sesame oil

¼ cup beef broth

½ cup of water

Method

1. Sprinkle the meat with ground black pepper, thyme, and sesame oil.

2. Then put it in the instant pot, add beef broth and water.

3. Close and seal the lid.

4. Cook the meal on manual mode (high pressure) for 25 minutes.

5. When the time is finished, make a quick pressure release.

Nutritional info per serve: calories 292, fat 14.4, fiber 0.3, carbs 0.7, protein 37.7

Lamb Kleftiko

Prep time: 25 minutes | **Cook time:** 50 minutes | **Yield:** 6 servings

Ingredients

1-pound lamb shoulder, chopped

½ cup turnip, chopped

1 tablespoon lemon juice

½ teaspoon lemon zest, grated

¼ cup apple cider vinegar

½ cup chicken broth

½ teaspoon fresh thyme

Method

1. In the mixing bowl, mix up lemon juice, lemon zest, apple cider vinegar, chicken broth, and thyme.

2. Then put the lamb shoulder in the instant pot.

3. Add lemon juice mixture and turnip.

4. Close and seal the lid.

5. Cook the meal on manual mode (high pressure) for 50 minutes.

6. When the time is over, allow the natural pressure release for 20 minutes.

Nutritional info per serve: calories 150, fat 5.7, fiber 0.2, carbs 1, protein 21.8

Lamb Bhuna

Prep time: 15 minutes | **Cook time:** 20 minutes | **Yield:** 2 servings

Ingredients

¼ teaspoon minced ginger

2 oz scallions, chopped

1 teaspoon coconut oil

10 oz lamb fillet, chopped

¼ teaspoon garlic paste

¼ cup crushed tomatoes

¼ cup of water

Method

1. Put the coconut oil, minced ginger, garlic paste, and crushed tomatoes in the instant pot.

2. Saute the mixture for 10 minutes.

3. Then stir it well and add scallions, chopped lamb fillet, and water.

4. Cook the lamb bhuna for 10 minutes on manual mode (high pressure).

5. When the time is finished, allow the natural pressure release for 15 minutes.

Nutritional info per serve: calories 306, fat 12.7, fiber 1.8, carbs 4.9, protein 41.1

Beef Vindaloo

Prep time: 15 minutes | **Cook time:** 15 minutes | **Yield:** 2 servings

Ingredients

½ serrano pepper, chopped

¼ teaspoon cumin seeds

9 oz beef clod, chopped

¼ teaspoon salt

¼ teaspoon ground paprika

¼ teaspoon minced ginger

1 cup of water

¼ teaspoon cayenne pepper

Method

1. Put serrano pepper, cumin seeds, salt, ground paprika, minced ginger, cayenne pepper, and water in the blender.

2. Blend the mixture till you get a smooth texture.

3. Then transfer it in the bowl and add chopped beef clod. Coat the meat in the blended mixture well.

4. Transfer the ingredients in the instant pot and close the lid.

5. Cook the meal on manual mode (high pressure) for 15 minutes.

6. Then allow the natural pressure release for 10 minutes.

Nutritional info per serve: calories 376, fat 27.4, fiber 0.3, carbs 0.7, protein 29.9

Lamb Masala

Prep time: 10 minutes | **Cook time:** 25 minutes | **Yield:** 3 servings

Ingredients

12 oz lamb sirloin, sliced

1 tablespoon garam masala

1 tablespoon lemon juice

1 tablespoon olive oil

¼ cup coconut cream

Method

1. Sprinkle the sliced lamb sirloin with garam masala, lemon juice, olive oil, and coconut cream. Mix up the meat mixture well and transfer it in the instant pot.

2. Cook it on saute mode for 25 minutes.

3. Stir the lamb masala every 5 minutes.

Nutritional info per serve: calories 319, fat 19.9, fiber 0.5, carbs 1.2, protein 32.7

Rogan Josh

Prep time: 5 minutes | **Cook time:** 15 minutes | **Yield:** 4 servings

Ingredients

1 teaspoon ground cardamom

½ teaspoon coriander powder

½ teaspoon ground turmeric

¼ teaspoon chili powder

1-pound lamb shoulder, boneless, chopped

½ cup organic almond milk

1 teaspoon tomato paste

1 teaspoon coconut oil

Method

1.   Put all ingredients in the instant pot and mix up.

2.   Then close and seal the lid.

3.   Cook the meal in manual mode for 15 minutes. Make a quick pressure release.

4.   Open the lid and stir the cooked Rogan Josh well. Top the cooked meal with chopped cilantro, if desired.

Nutritional info per serve: calories 232, fat 9.9, fiber 0.3, carbs 1.9, protein 32.1

Icelandic Lamb

Prep time: 5 minutes | **Cook time:** 45 minutes | **Yield:** 4 servings

Ingredients

3 oz celery ribs, chopped

¼ cup scallions, chopped

4 oz turnip, chopped

1 teaspoon tomato paste

½ teaspoon ground black pepper

½ teaspoon salt

4 cups of water

12 oz lamb fillet, chopped

Method

1.   Put all ingredients in the instant pot and stir well until the tomato paste is dissolved.

2.   Then close and seal the lid.

3.   Cook the lamb on manual (high pressure) for 45 minutes.

4.   Then make the quick pressure release, open the lid, and mix up the lamb well.

Nutritional info per serve: calories 173, fat 6.3, fiber 1.1, carbs 3.3, protein 24.5

Harissa Lamb Shoulder

Prep time: 30 minutes | **Cook time:** 40 minutes | **Yield:** 4 servings

Ingredients

16 oz lamb shoulder

1 tablespoon harissa

2 tablespoons sesame oil

2 cups of water

1 teaspoon dried thyme

½ teaspoon salt

Method

1.   In the shallow bowl mix up harissa and dried thyme.

2.   Then rub the lamb shoulder with the spice mixture and brush with sesame oil.

3.   Heat up the instant pot on saute mode for 2 minutes and put the lamb shoulder inside.

4.   Cook the meat for 3 minutes from each side. Add water.

5.   Close and seal the lid.

6.   Cook it on manual mode (high pressure) for 40 minutes.

7.   When the cooking time is finished, allow the natural pressure release for 25 minutes.

Nutritional info per serve: calories 284, fat 15.8, fiber 0.1, carbs 1.7, protein 32.1

Kofta Curry

Prep time: 15 minutes | **Cook time:** 20 minutes | **Yield:** 4 servings

Ingredients

1-pound ground lamb

1 tablespoon curry powder

1/3 cup coconut cream

4 oz scallions, chopped

1 cup chicken broth

1 tablespoon dried cilantro

½ teaspoon chili flakes

1 tablespoon coconut oil

Method

1.   In the mixing bowl, mix up ½ tablespoon of curry powder, scallions, and ground lamb.

2.   Add chili flakes and dried cilantro. Stir the mixture until homogenous and make the medium size koftas (meatballs).

3.   Then heat up the coconut oil until it is melted (saute mode).

4.   Put the koftas in the hot oil and cook them for 2 minutes from each side.

5.   Then mix up coconut cream and remaining curry powder. Add chicken broth and pour the liquid over the koftas.

6.   Cook the meal on manual (high pressure) for 12 minutes. Allow the natural pressure release for 10 minutes.

Nutritional info per serve: calories 310, fat 17.1, fiber 1.7, carbs 4.4, protein 34.2

Pesto Rack of Lamb

Prep time: 15 minutes | **Cook time:** 45 minutes | **Yield:** 4 servings

Ingredients

2 tablespoons pesto sauce

1 tablespoon coconut oil

1 teaspoon chili powder

1-pound rack of lamb

1 cup of water

Method

1.   Rub the rack of lamb with pesto sauce and chili powder. Leave the meat for 15 minutes to marinate.

2.   Then heat up coconut oil on saute mode for 3 minutes.

3.   Put the marinated lamb in the hot oil and cook it on saute mode for 4 minutes from each side.

4.   Then add water. Close and seal the lid.

5.   Cook the lamb on manual (high pressure) for 45 minutes. Make a quick pressure release.

Nutritional info per serve: calories 256, fat 16.8, fiber 0.4, carbs 0.9, protein 23.9

Koobideh

Prep time: 15 minutes | **Cook time:** 30 minutes | **Yield:** 4 servings

Ingredients

1-pound ground lamb

1 teaspoon ground turmeric

½ teaspoon ground black pepper

1 tablespoon lemon juice

1 teaspoon chives, chopped

½ teaspoon garlic powder

1 egg, beaten

1 cup water, for cooking

Method

1. In the mixing bowl mix up all ingredients from the list above.

2. Then make the meatballs and press them well to get the shape of an ellipse.

3. Then pour water and insert the steamer rack in the instant pot.

4. Put the prepared ellipse meatballs in the baking mold and transfer it on the steamer rack.

5. Close and seal the lid and cook the meal on manual mode (high pressure) for 30 minutes. Make a quick pressure release.

Nutritional info per serve: calories 231, fat 9.5, fiber 0.3, carbs 1, protein 33.4

Shami Kabob

Prep time: 15 minutes | **Cook time:** 40 minutes | **Yield:** 4 servings

Ingredients

1-pound beef chunks

¼ cup almond flour

1 teaspoon ginger paste

½ teaspoon ground cumin

2 cups of water

1 tablespoon coconut oil

1 egg, beaten

Method

1. Chop the beef chunks and put them in the instant pot.

2. Add ginger paste, ground cumin, and water.

3. Cook the meat on manual mode (high pressure) for 30 minutes. Make a quick pressure release.

4. Drain the water from the meat.

5. Then transfer the beef in the blender. Add almond flour. Blend the ingredients until smooth. Make the small meatballs.

6. Heat up coconut oil on saute mode and put the meatballs inside.

7. Cook them for 2 minutes from each side or until golden brown.

Nutritional info per serve: calories 179, fat 9.5, fiber 0.3, carbs 2.9, protein 20.1

Lamb Burger

Prep time: 10 minutes | **Cook time:** 14 minutes | **Yield:** 2 servings

Ingredients

10 oz ground lamb

1 teaspoon garlic powder

½ teaspoon chili powder

1 teaspoon dried cilantro

½ teaspoon salt

¼ cup of water

1 tablespoon coconut oil

Method

1. In the mixing bowl, mix up ground lamb, garlic powder, chili powder, dried cilantro, salt, and water.

2. Make 2 burgers from the lamb mixture.

3. Melt the coconut oil on saute mode.

4. Then put the burgers in the hot oil and cook them for 7 minutes from each side.

Nutritional info per serve: calories 329, fat 17.3, fiber 0.4, carbs 1.4, protein 40.1

Steamed Rostelle

Prep time: 20 minutes | **Cook time:** 30 minutes | **Yield:** 4 servings

Ingredients

1-pound lamb loin

1 teaspoon ground black pepper

1 teaspoon olive oil

½ teaspoon apple cider vinegar

½ teaspoon salt

1 cup water, for cooking

Method

1.   Slice the lamb loin into the medium size strips and sprinkle with ground black pepper, olive oil, apple cider vinegar, and salt.

2.   Mix up the meat well.

3.   Then sting it on the skewers and put in the baking pan.

4.   Pour water in the instant pot and then insert the steamer rack.

5.   Put the baking mold with skewers on the rack. Close and seal the lid.

6.   Cook the meal on manual (high pressure) for 30 minutes. Allow the natural pressure release for 10 minutes.

Nutritional info per serve: calories 241, fat 12.3, fiber 0.1, carbs 0.4, protein 30.2

Veal Meatloaf

Prep time: 20 minutes | **Cook time:** 25 minutes | **Yield:** 4 servings

Ingredients

1-pound veal, minced

1 tablespoon mustard

2 eggs, beaten

¼ cup coconut flour

1 teaspoon salt

1 teaspoon ground cumin

1 teaspoon olive oil

1 cup water, for cooking

Method

1.   In the mixing bowl, mix up minced veal, mustard, eggs, coconut flour, salt, and ground cumin.

2.   Then brush the baking mold with olive oil.

3.   Put the ground veal mixture in the mold and press it gently to get the shape of a loaf.

4.   Then pour water and insert the steamer rack in the instant pot.

5.   Put the mold with meatloaf on the rack. Close and seal the lid.

6.   Cook the meatloaf on manual mode (high pressure) for 25 minutes. Allow the natural pressure release for 15 minutes.

Nutritional info per serve: calories 281, fat 13.6, fiber 3.5, carbs 6.4, protein 32.2

Peppered Lamb Ribs

Prep time: 20 minutes | **Cook time:** 35 minutes | **Yield:** 4 servings

Ingredients

1-pound lamb ribs, chopped

1 teaspoon peppercorn, grinded

¼ cup apple cider vinegar

2 tablespoons coconut aminos

1 teaspoon cumin seeds

1 cup of water

Method

1. Put all ingredients in the instant pot.

2. Close and seal the lid.

3. Cook the meat on manual mode (high pressure) for 35 minutes.

4. Then allow the natural pressure release for 15 minutes.

5. Serve the lamb ribs with hot gravy from the instant pot.

Nutritional info per serve: calories 205, fat 10.2, fiber 0.2, carbs 2.2, protein 23.2

PORK

Pork Chops with Blue Cheese

Prep time: 5 minutes | **Cook time:** 20 minutes | **Yield:** 2 servings

Ingredients

2 pork chops

2 oz blue cheese, crumbled

1 teaspoon coconut oil

1 teaspoon lemon juice

¼ cup heavy cream

Method

1. Heat up coconut oil in the instant pot on saute mode.

2. Then put the pork chops in the instant pot and cook them on saute mode for 5 minutes from each side.

3. Then add lemon juice and crumbled cheese.

4. Stir the ingredients well.

5. Add heavy cream and close the lid.

6. Cook the pork chops on saute mode for 10 minutes more.

Nutritional info per serve: calories 300, fat 25.9, fiber 0, carbs 1.1, protein 15.4

Carnitas Pulled Pork

Prep time: 20 minutes | **Cook time:** 45 minutes | **Yield:** 5 servings

Ingredients

1-pound pork shoulder, boneless

½ teaspoon minced garlic

½ teaspoon ground cumin

2 tablespoons butter

1 chili pepper, chopped

½ teaspoon lime zest, grated

1 ½ cup beef broth

Method

1. Put all ingredients in the instant pot.

2. Close and seal the lid.

3. Cook the pork for 45 minutes on manual mode (high pressure).

4. Then allow the natural pressure release for 10 minutes and open the lid.

5. Shred the cooked pork with the help of the forks and transfer in the bowl.

6. Add ½ part of all remaining liquid and stir the pulled pork.

Nutritional info per serve: calories 319, fat 24.5, fiber 0.1, carbs 0.6, protein 22.7

Sweet Pork Tenderloin

Prep time: 15 minutes | **Cook time:** 30 minutes | **Yield:** 2 servings

Ingredients

9 oz pork tenderloin

1 teaspoon Erythritol

½ teaspoon dried dill

½ teaspoon white pepper

1 garlic clove, minced

3 tablespoons butter

¼ cup of water

Method

1.   Rub the pork tenderloin with Erythritol, dried dill, white pepper, and minced garlic.

2.   Then melt the butter in the instant pot on saute mode.

3.   Add pork tenderloin and cook it for 8 minutes from each side (use saute mode).

4.   Then add water and close the lid.

5.   Cook the meat on saute mode for 10 minutes.

6.   Cool the cooked tenderloin for 10-15 minutes and slice.

Nutritional info per serve: calories 339, fat 21.8, fiber 0.2, carbs 3.5, protein 33.8

Thyme Pork Meatballs

Prep time: 15 minutes | **Cook time:** 16 minutes | **Yield:** 8 servings

Ingredients

2 cups ground pork

1 teaspoon dried thyme

½ teaspoon chili flakes

½ teaspoon garlic powder

1 tablespoon coconut oil

¼ teaspoon ground ginger

3 tablespoons almond flour

¼ cup of water

Method

1.   In the mixing bowl, mix up ground pork, dried thyme, chili flakes, garlic powder, ground ginger, and almond flour.

2.   Make the meatballs.

3.   Melt the coconut oil in the instant pot on saute mode.

4.   Arrange the meatballs in the instant pot in one layer and cook them for 3 minutes from each side.

5.   Then add water and cook the meatballs for 10 minutes.

Nutritional info per serve: calories 264, fat 19.2, fiber 0.4, carbs 0.8, protein 20.7

Asian Ribs

Prep time: 15 minutes | **Cook time:** 25 minutes | **Yield:** 3 servings

Ingredients

¼ teaspoon ground cardamom

½ teaspoon minced ginger

4 tablespoons apple cider vinegar

¼ teaspoon sesame seeds

10 oz pork ribs, chopped

¼ teaspoon chili flakes

1 tablespoon avocado oil

Method

1.   In the mixing bowl, mix up ground cardamom. Minced ginger, apple cider vinegar, sesame seeds, chili flakes, and avocado oil.

2.   Then brush the pork ribs with the cardamom mixture and leave for 10 minutes to marinate.

3.   After this, heat up the instant pot on saute mode for 2 minutes.

4.   Add the marinated pork ribs and all remaining marinade.

5.   Cook the pork ribs on saute mode for 25 minutes. Flip the ribs on another side every 5 minutes.

Nutritional info per serve: calories 271, fat 17.5, fiber 0.3, carbs 0.9, protein 25.2

Mississippi Pork

Prep time: 10 minutes | **Cook time:** 6 hours | **Yield:** 7 servings

Ingredients

1 tablespoon ranch dressing mix

1 ½ pound pork butt roast, chopped

1 cup butter

1 chili pepper, chopped

½ cup of water

Method

1. Put all ingredients in the instant pot.

2. Close the instant pot and cook the meal for 6 hours on low pressure.

3. When the time is over, shred the meat gently and transfer in the serving plate.

Nutritional info per serve: calories 414, fat 38.4, fiber 0, carbs 0.2, protein 17.5

BBQ Baby Back Ribs

Prep time: 10 minutes | **Cook time:** 30 minutes | **Yield:** 4 servings

Ingredients

1-pound pork baby back ribs, chopped

¼ cup keto BBQ sauce

½ cup of water

1 tablespoon sesame seeds

Method

1. Put the chopped ribs, BBQ sauce, and sesame seeds in the instant pot. Add water.

2. Close and seal the lid.

3. Cook the meal on manual mode (high pressure) for 30 minutes.

4. Then allow the natural pressure release for 10 minutes.

Nutritional info per serve: calories 450, fat 34.9, fiber 0.4, carbs 6.2, protein 26.1

Vietnamese Pork

Prep time: 10 minutes | **Cook time:** 20 minutes | **Yield:** 2 servings

Ingredients

6 oz pork tenderloin

½ cup of water

¼ teaspoon ground clove

¼ teaspoon minced ginger

1 teaspoon coconut aminos

1 teaspoon olive oil

Method

1. Heat up olive oil on saute mode.

2. Then chop the pork tenderloin roughly and add it in the instant pot.

3. Cook the meat for 2 minutes and flip it on another side.

4. After this, add coconut aminos, minced ginger, ground clove, and water.

5. Close and seal the lid and cook the meat on manual (high pressure) for 15 minutes.

6. Allow the natural pressure release for 10 minutes and transfer the meat in the bowls.

Nutritional info per serve: calories 146, fat 5.4, fiber 0.1, carbs 0.8, protein 22.3

Pork Tenders

Prep time: 10 minutes | **Cook time:** 20 minutes | **Yield:** 6 servings

Ingredients

1-pound pork tenderloin, sliced

½ cup apple cider vinegar

1 teaspoon ground nutmeg

1 tablespoon butter

½ cup of water

Method

1.   Mix up the sliced pork tenderloin with ground nutmeg and put it in the instant pot.

2.   Add water, butter, and apple cider vinegar.

3.   Close and seal the lid and cook the meat on manual mode (high pressure) for 20 minutes.

4.   When the time is finished, make a quick pressure release and open the lid.

Nutritional info per serve: calories 131, fat 4.7, fiber 0.1, carbs 0.4, protein 19.8

Stuffed Pork Rolls

Prep time: 15 minutes | **Cook time:** 21 minutes | **Yield:** 4 servings

Ingredients

¼ cup almonds, chopped

12 oz pork fillet

¼ cup spinach

2 oz Parmesan

1 tablespoon avocado oil

5 tablespoons beef broth

Method

1.   Cut the pork fillet on 4 fillets and beat them with the help of the kitchen hammer.

2.   Blend the spinach until smooth.

3.   After this, grate Parmesan and mix it up with blended spinach and chopped almonds.

4.   Sprinkle the spinach mixture over the fillets and roll them in the "envelops".

5.   Heat up avocado oil on saute mode.

6.   Place the pork rolls in the hot oil and cook them on saute mode for 3 minutes from each side.

7.   After this, add water and cook the meal with the closed lid for 15 minutes. Flip the rolls on another side every 5 minutes to avoid burning.

Nutritional info per serve: calories 286, fat 17.4, fiber 0.9, carbs 2.1, protein 29.9

Aromatic Pork Belly

Prep time: 10 minutes | **Cook time:** 75 minutes | **Yield:** 4 servings

Ingredients

10 oz pork belly

1 teaspoon dried rosemary

½ teaspoon dried thyme

¼ teaspoon ground cinnamon

1 teaspoon salt

1 cup of water

Method

1.   Rub the pork belly with dried rosemary, thyme, ground cinnamon, and salt and transfer in the instant pot bowl.

2.   Add water, close and seal the lid.

3.   Cook the pork belly on manual mode (high pressure) for 75 minutes.

4.   Remove the cooked pork belly from the instant pot and slice it into servings.

Nutritional info per serve: calories 329, fat 19.1, fiber 0.3, carbs 0.4, protein 32.7

Ranch Pork Chops

Prep time: 15 minutes | **Cook time:** 15 minutes | **Yield:** 4 servings

Ingredients

1 teaspoon ranch seasonings

1 tablespoon olive oil

4 pork chops

1 cup of water

Method

1.   Rub the pork chops with ranch seasonings and olive oil.

2.   Then place the meat in the instant pot, add water. Close and seal the lid.

3.   Cook the pork chops on manual mode (high pressure) for 15 minutes.

4.   Naturally release the pressure and transfer the meat on the plates.

Nutritional info per serve: calories 289, fat 23.4, fiber 0, carbs 0, protein 18

Paprika Ribs

Prep time: 10 minutes | **Cook time:** 30 minutes | **Yield:** 4 servings

Ingredients

1-pound pork ribs

1 tablespoon ground paprika

1 teaspoon ground turmeric

3 tablespoons avocado oil

1 teaspoon salt

½ cup beef broth

Method

1.   Rub the pork ribs with ground paprika, turmeric, salt, and avocado oil.

2.   Then pour the beef broth in the instant pot.

3.   Arrange the pork ribs in the instant pot. Close and seal the lid.

4.   Cook the pork ribs for 30 minutes on manual mode (high pressure).

5.   When the time is finished, make a quick pressure release and chop the ribs into servings.

Nutritional info per serve: calories 335, fat 21.9, fiber 1.2, carbs 2, protein 31.1

Wrapped Pork Cubes

Prep time: 15 minutes | **Cook time:** 20 minutes | **Yield:** 4 servings

Ingredients

6 oz bacon, sliced

10 oz pork tenderloin, cubed

½ teaspoon white pepper

3 tablespoons butter

¾ cup chicken stock

Method

1.   Melt the butter on saute mode.

2.   Meanwhile, wrap the pork tenderloin cubes in the sliced bacon and sprinkle with white pepper.

3.   Put the wrapped pork tenderloin in the melted butter and cook them for 3 minutes from each side.

4.   Add chicken stock and close the lid.

5.   Cook the pork cubes on saute mode for 14 minutes or until meat is tender.

Nutritional info per serve: calories 410, fat 29, fiber 0.1, carbs 0.9, protein 34.6

Herbed Pork Tenderloin

Prep time: 15 minutes | **Cook time:** 18 minutes | **Yield:** 4 servings

Ingredients

¼ teaspoon ground cumin

½ teaspoon ground nutmeg

½ teaspoon dried thyme

½ teaspoon ground coriander

1 tablespoon sesame oil

1-pound pork tenderloin

2 tablespoons apple cider vinegar

1 cup of water

Method

1.   In the mixing bowl, mix up ground cumin, ground nutmeg, thyme, ground coriander, and apple cider vinegar.

2.   Then rub the meat with the spice mixture.

3.   Heat up sesame oil on saute mode for 2 minutes.

4.   Put the pork tenderloin in the hot oil and cook it for 5 minutes from each side or until meat is light brown.

5.   Add water.

6.   Close and seal the lid. Cook the meat on manual mode (high pressure) for 5 minutes.

7.   When the time is finished, allow the natural pressure release for 15 minutes.

Nutritional info per serve: calories 196, fat 7.5, fiber 0.1, carbs 0.4, protein 29.7

Cilantro Pork Shoulder

Prep time: 10 minutes | **Cook time:** 85 minutes | **Yield:** 4 servings

Ingredients

1-pound pork shoulder, boneless

¼ cup fresh cilantro, chopped

1 cup of water

1 teaspoon salt

1 teaspoon coconut oil

½ teaspoon mustard seeds

Method

1.   Pour water in the instant pot.

2.   Add pork shoulder, fresh cilantro, salt, coconut oil, and mustard seeds.

3.   Close and seal the lid. Cook the meat on high pressure (manual mode) for 85 minutes.

4.   Then make a quick pressure release and open the lid.

5.   The cooked meat has to be served with the remaining liquid from the instant pot.

Nutritional info per serve: calories 343, fat 25.5, fiber 0.1, carbs 0.2, protein 26.5

Peppercorn Pork

Prep time: 10 minutes | **Cook time:** 12 minutes | **Yield:** 3 servings

Ingredients

3 pork chops

1 tablespoon mascarpone cheese

1 teaspoon peppercorns, grinded

½ teaspoon dried sage

1 tablespoon sunflower oil

Method

1.   In the shallow bowl, mix up peppercorns, dried sage, sunflower oil, and mascarpone cheese.

2. Brush the pork chops with the cheese mixture well and transfer in the instant pot.

3. Cook the meat on saute mode for 5 minutes from each side.

4. Then add the remaining cream cheese mixture and cook the pork chops for 2 minutes more.

Nutritional info per serve: calories 308, fat 25.3, fiber 0.2, carbs 0.7, protein 18.7

Pork Ragu

Prep time: 10 minutes | **Cook time:** 15 minutes | **Yield:** 3 servings

Ingredients

1 bell pepper, sliced

½ zucchini, chopped

1 daikon, sliced

7 oz pork chops, sliced

1 teaspoon almond butter

½ cup coconut cream

½ teaspoon cayenne pepper

Method

1. Melt the almond butter in the instant pot on saute mode.

2. Add sliced pork chops and sprinkle them with cayenne pepper.

3. Cook the meat for 5 minutes.

4. Then flip it on another side and add chopped zucchini and sliced bell pepper.

5. Add daikon and coconut cream.

6. Close and seal the lid.

7. Cook the pork ragu on high pressure (manual mode) for 10 minutes. Make a quick pressure release.

Nutritional info per serve: calories 359, fat 29.2, fiber 2.7, carbs 8.2, protein 18.1

Apple Cider Vinegar Ham

Prep time: 10 minutes | **Cook time:** 10 minutes | **Yield:** 6 servings

Ingredients

1-pound bone-in ham, cooked

1 cup apple cider vinegar

2 tablespoons Erythritol

2 tablespoons butter

1 tablespoon avocado oil

½ teaspoon pumpkin pie spices

Method

1. Pour apple cider vinegar in the instant pot and insert the steamer rack.

2. Then rub the ham with Erythritol, butter, avocado oil, and pumpkin pie spices.

3. Put the ham on the rack. Close and seal the lid.

4. Cook the ham on high pressure (manual mode) for 10 minutes.

5. Allow the natural pressure release for 5 minutes and open the lid.

6. Slice the ham.

Nutritional info per serve: calories 134, fat 5.4, fiber 0.1, carbs 6.9, protein 16.5

Smothered Pork Chops

Prep time: 10 minutes | **Cook time:** 17 minutes | **Yield:** 4 servings

Ingredients

4 pork chops

1 teaspoon pork seasonings

½ teaspoon ground black pepper

¼ cup heavy cream

½ cup chicken broth

1 teaspoon olive oil

Method

1.   Heat up olive oil on saute mode for 1 minute.

2.   Then place the pork chops in the instant pot and cook them for 3 minutes from each side or until they are light brown.

3.   Sprinkle the meat with pork seasonings, ground black pepper, chicken broth, and heavy cream.

4.   Close and seal the lid.

5.   Cook the meal for 10 minutes on manual mode (high pressure).

6.   Make a quick pressure release.

Nutritional info per serve: calories 298, fat 24, fiber 0.1, carbs 0.6, protein 18.8

Meatloaf with Eggs

Prep time: 20 minutes | **Cook time:** 25 minutes | **Yield:** 6 servings

Ingredients

1 ½ cup ground pork

1 teaspoon chives

1 teaspoon salt

½ teaspoon ground black pepper

3 eggs, hard-boiled, peeled

2 tablespoons coconut flour

1 tablespoon avocado oil

1 cup water, for cooking

Method

1.   Brush the loaf mold with avocado oil.

2.   After this, in the mixing bowl, mix up ground pork, chives, salt, ground black pepper, and coconut flour.

3.   Transfer the mixture in the loaf mold and flatten well.

4.   Fill it with hard-boiled eggs.

5.   Pour water and insert the steamer rack in the instant pot.

6.   Put the meatloaf in the instant pot. Close and seal the lid.

7.   Cook the meal on manual (high pressure) for 25 minutes. Allow the natural pressure release for 10 minutes.

Nutritional info per serve: calories 277, fat 19, fiber 1.2, carbs 2.1, protein 23.3

Turmeric Pork Strips

Prep time: 10 minutes | **Cook time:** 22 minutes | **Yield:** 4 servings

Ingredients

1-pound pork loin

1 teaspoon ground turmeric

1 teaspoon coconut oil

½ teaspoon salt

½ cup organic almond milk

Method

1. Cut the pork loin into the strips and sprinkle with salt and ground turmeric.

2. Heat up the coconut oil on saute mode for 1 minute and add pork strips.

3. Saute them for 6 minutes. Stir the meat from time to time.

4. After this, add almond milk and close the lid.

5. Saute the pork for 15 minutes.

Nutritional info per serve: calories 226, fat 11, fiber 0.1, carbs 1.4, protein 30.5

Fabulous Cilantro Meatballs

Prep time: 10 minutes | **Cook time:** 15 minutes | **Yield:** 3 servings

Ingredients

1 cup ground pork

1 oz fresh cilantro, chopped

1 garlic clove, diced

½ teaspoon salt

1 teaspoon ground coriander

2 tablespoons butter

1 tablespoon coconut cream

Method

1. Blend the fresh cilantro until it is smooth and mix it up with ground pork, diced garlic, salt, and ground coriander.

2. Make the small meatballs and press them gently with the help of the hand palms.

3. Then melt the butter in the instant pot on saute mode and add the meatballs.

4. Cook them for 3 minutes from each side. Add coconut cream and close the lid.

5. Cook the meal on saute mode for 5 minutes.

Nutritional info per serve: calories 393, fat 30.6, fiber 0.4, carbs 1, protein 27.3

Basil Pork Loin

Prep time: 10 minutes | **Cook time:** 17 minutes | **Yield:** 4 servings

Ingredients

1-pound pork loin

1 teaspoon dried basil

1 tablespoon avocado oil

1 teaspoon dried thyme

½ teaspoon salt

2 tablespoons apple cider vinegar

1 cup water, for cooking

Method

1. In the shallow bowl, mix up dried basil, avocado oil, thyme, salt, and apple cider vinegar.

2. Then rub the pork loin with the spice mixture and leave the meat for 10 minutes to marinate.

3. Wrap the meat in foil and put on the steamer rack.

4. Pour water and transfer the steamer rack with meat in the instant pot.

5. Close and seal the lid. Cook the meat on manual (high pressure) for 20 minutes. Allow the natural pressure release for 5 minutes.

6. Slice the cooked pork loin.

Nutritional info per serve: calories 281, fat 16.3, fiber 0.2, carbs 0.4, protein 31.1

Ground Pork Stroganoff

Prep time: 10 minutes | **Cook time:** 25 minutes | **Yield:** 4 servings

Ingredients

½ cup cremini mushrooms, chopped

1 teaspoon dried oregano

½ teaspoon ground nutmeg

½ cup of coconut milk

1 cup ground pork

½ teaspoon salt

2 tablespoons butter

Method

1.   Heat up butter on saute mode for 3 minutes.

2.   Add mushrooms. Saute the vegetables for 5 minutes.

3.   Then stir them and add salt, ground pork, ground nutmeg, and dried oregano.

4.   Stir the ingredients and cook for 5 minutes more.

5.   Add coconut milk and close the lid.

6.   Saute the stroganoff for 15 minutes. Stir it from time to time to avoid burning.

Nutritional info per serve: calories 357, fat 29.3, fiber 0.9, carbs 2.4, protein 21.1

Stew Cubes

Prep time: 15 minutes | **Cook time:** 25 minutes | **Yield:** 2 servings

Ingredients

10 oz pork tenderloin

1 teaspoon tomato paste

1 bay leaf

1 teaspoon salt

1 cup of water

1 teaspoon allspices

1 teaspoon coconut oil

Method

1.   Cut the pork tenderloin into the cubes and sprinkle with salt and allspices.

2.   Then heat up the coconut oil in the instant pot on saute mode. Add pork cubes.

3.   Roast the meat for 2 minutes per side.

4.   Add tomato paste and water.

5.   Close and seal the lid.

6.   Cook the stew cubes for 25 minutes on manual mode (high pressure).

7.   When the cooking time is finished, allow the natural pressure release for 10 minutes.

Nutritional info per serve: calories 229, fat 7.4, fiber 0.5, carbs 1.6, protein 37.3

Pork Milanese

Prep time: 10 minutes | **Cook time:** 20 minutes | **Yield:** 2 servings

Ingredients

2 bone-in pork chops

1 teaspoon salt

1 teaspoon ground black pepper

½ cup coconut flakes

1 oz Parmesan, grated

2 eggs, beaten

1 teaspoon onion powder

1/3 cup butter

Method

1.   Rub the pork chops with salt and ground black pepper.

2. In the mixing bowl, mix up coconut flakes, onion powder, and grated Parmesan.

3. Then dip the pork chops in the beaten eggs and coat in the coconut flakes mixture.

4. Melt the butter in the instant pot on saute mode.

5. Add the pork chops and cook them for 10 minutes from each side.

Nutritional info per serve: calories 697, fat 56.8, fiber 2.2, carbs 6.6, protein 40.3

Romano Pork Chops

Prep time: 10 minutes | **Cook time:** 18 minutes | **Yield:** 3 servings

Ingredients

3 pork chops

4 oz Romano cheese, grated

½ teaspoon Cajun seasoning

1 egg, beaten

1 tablespoon cream cheese

1/3 cup almond flour

3 tablespoons avocado oil

Method

1. Rub the pork chops with Cajun seasonings.

2. After this, in the mixing bowl mix up grated Romano cheese and almond flour.

3. In the separated bow mix up eggs and cream cheese.

4. Dip the pork chops in the egg mixture and then coat in the cheese mixture.

5. Repeat the step one more time.

6. Pour avocado oil in the instant pot. Preheat it on saute mode for 2 minutes.

7. Add the pork chops and cook them for 8 minutes per side.

Nutritional info per serve: calories 528, fat 40.4, fiber 1.9, carbs 5, protein 35

Ground Pork Pizza Crust

Prep time: 10 minutes | **Cook time:** 15 minutes | **Yield:** 4 servings

Ingredients

½ cup Cheddar cheese, shredded

1 cup ground pork

1 teaspoon Italian seasonings

1 tablespoon Psyllium husk

1 teaspoon olive oil

1 cup water, for cooking

Method

1. In the mixing bowl, mix up shredded cheese, ground pork, Italian seasonings, and Psyllium husk.

2. Line the round instant pot pan with baking paper and brush with olive oil.

3. Then put the ground pork mixture in the pan and flatten it in the shape of the pizza crust.

4. Pour water and insert the steamer rack in the instant pot.

5. Put the pan with pizza crust on the rack. Close and seal the lid.

6. Cook the meal on manual mode (high pressure) for 15 minutes. Make a quick pressure release.

Nutritional info per serve: calories 324, fat 22.5, fiber 7, carbs 8.8, protein 23.6

Pork Chops Al Pastor

Prep time: 10 minutes | **Cook time:** 30 minutes | **Yield:** 4 servings

Ingredients

4 pork chops

1 teaspoon Achiote paste

1 teaspoon minced garlic

1 tablespoon avocado oil

2 tablespoon lime juice

½ cup chicken broth

Method

1.   In the shallow bowl, mix up Achiote paste, minced garlic, avocado oil, and lime juice.

2.   Then rub the pork chops with the Achiote paste mixture and put in the instant pot.

3.   Cook the meat on Saute mode for 6 minutes from each side.

4.   Add chicken broth and close the lid.

5.   Cook the meal on Saute mode for 20 minutes.

Nutritional info per serve: calories 279, fat 21.5, fiber 0.2, carbs 1.1, protein 18.9

Taco Casserole

Prep time: 20 minutes | **Cook time:** 30 minutes | **Yield:** 4 servings

Ingredients

1 cup ground pork

1 tablespoon taco seasonings

1 tablespoon coconut oil

½ teaspoon dried cilantro

¼ cup Cheddar cheese, shredded

½ cup beef broth

Method

1.   In the mixing bowl, mix up ground pork, taco seasonings, and dried cilantro.

2.   Then grease the casserole mold with coconut oil and put the pork mixture inside. Flatten it well.

3.   After this, top the casserole mixture with shredded cheese.

4.   Add beef broth and cover the casserole with foil.

5.   Pour water in the instant pot and place the casserole inside.

6.   Close and seal the lid.

7.   Cook the meal on manual (high pressure) for 30 minutes.

8.   Allow the natural pressure release for 10 minutes.

Nutritional info per serve: calories 302, fat 22.2, fiber 0, carbs 1.7, protein 22.5

Mozzarella Stuffed Meatballs

Prep time: 10 minutes | **Cook time:** 20 minutes | **Yield:** 6 servings

Ingredients

1-pound ground pork

1 teaspoon chili flakes

½ teaspoon salt

1/3 cup Mozzarella, shredded

1 tablespoon butter

¼ cup chicken broth

½ teaspoon garlic powder

Method

1.   Mix up ground pork, chili flakes, salt, and garlic powder.

2. Then make the meatballs with the help of the fingertips.

3. Make the mini balls from the cheese.

4. Fill the meatballs with the mini cheese balls.

5. Toss the butter in the instant pot.

6. Heat it up on saute mode and add the prepared meatballs.

7. Cook the on saute mode for 3 minutes from each side.

8. Then add chicken broth and close the lid.

9. Cook the meal on meat/stew mode for 10 minutes.

Nutritional info per serve: calories 132, fat 4.9, fiber 0, carbs 0.3, protein 20.5

Smoked Sausages Cabbage

Prep time: 15 minutes | **Cook time:** 20 minutes | **Yield:** 2 servings

Ingredients

1 cup white cabbage, shredded

6 oz smoked sausages, chopped

1 teaspoon avocado oil

1 teaspoon ground paprika

½ teaspoon chili powder

1 cup chicken stock

Method

1. Put the smoked sausages and avocado oil in the instant pot and cook the ingredients on saute mode for 5 minutes. Stir them from time to time.

2. After this, add ground paprika, chili powder, and shredded cabbage. Mix up well.

3. Add chicken stock. Close and seal the lid.

4. Cook the meal on manual mode (high pressure) for 15 minutes.

5. Then make a quick pressure release.

6. Stir the meal well before serving.

Nutritional info per serve: calories 310, fat 25, fiber 1.6, carbs 3.5, protein 17.6

Sub Salad

Prep time: 10 minutes | **Cook time:** 15 minutes | **Yield:** 4 servings

Ingredients

1 tomato, chopped

1/3 cup black olives, sliced

1 cup lettuce, chopped

1 tablespoon olive oil

½ teaspoon chicken seasonings

10 oz pork fillet

1/3 cup water, for cooking

Method

1. Slice the pork fillet and sprinkle with chicken seasonings.

2. Then place the sliced meat in the instant pot, add olive oil and cook on saute mode for 5 minutes.

3. Stir it from time to time.

4. When the meat is light brown, add water and close the lid.

5. Cook it on meat/stew mode for 10 minutes.

6. Meanwhile, in the salad bowl, mix up tomato, black olives, and lettuce.

7. Top the salad with the cooked pork slices.

Nutritional info per serve: calories 213, fat 13.8, fiber 0.6, carbs 1.7, protein 20

POULTRY

Garlic Chicken with Lemon

Prep time: 20 minutes | **Cook time:** 30 minutes | **Yield:** 6 servings

Ingredients

2-pound chicken thighs, skinless

1 tablespoon avocado oil

1 teaspoon minced garlic

½ teaspoon ground coriander

1 teaspoon lemon zest

1 teaspoon lemon juice

1/3 cup chicken broth

1 cup of water

Method

1.   Pour water and insert the steamer rack in the instant pot. Pour water and chicken broth in the instant pot bowl.

2.   Put the chicken thighs in the bowl and sprinkle them with avocado oil, minced garlic, ground coriander, lemon zest, and lemon juice.

3.   Then shake the chicken thighs gently and transfer them on the steamer rack.

4.   Close and seal the lid.

5.   Cook the chicken for 15 minutes on manual mode (high pressure).

6.   Then make a quick pressure release and transfer the chicken thighs on the plate.

Nutritional info per serve: calories 294, fat 11.6, fiber 0.1, carbs 0.4, protein 44.1

Tuscan Chicken

Prep time: 15 minutes | **Cook time:** 12 minutes | **Yield:** 4 servings

Ingredients

4 chicken drumsticks

1 cup spinach, chopped

1 teaspoon minced garlic

1 teaspoon ground paprika

1 cup heavy cream

1 teaspoon cayenne pepper

1 oz sun-dried tomatoes, chopped

Method

1.   Put all ingredients in the instant pot.

2.   Close and seal the lid.

3.   Cook the meal on manual mode (high pressure) for 12 minutes.

4.   Then allow the natural pressure release for 10 minutes.

5.   Serve the chicken with hot sauce from the instant pot.

Nutritional info per serve: calories 188, fat 13.9, fiber 0.6, carbs 2.2, protein 13.7

Crack Chicken

Prep time: 15 minutes | **Cook time:** 20 minutes | **Yield:** 4 servings

Ingredients

1 cup chicken broth

1 teaspoon dried dill

1 teaspoon dried oregano

½ teaspoon onion powder

1-pound chicken breast, skinless, boneless

½ teaspoon salt

2 tablespoons mascarpone cheese

2 oz Cheddar cheese, shredded

Method

1. Pour the chicken broth in the instant pot.

2. Add dried ill, oregano, onion powder, chicken breast, and salt.

3. Close and seal the lid.

4. Cook the chicken breast on manual mode (high pressure) for 15 minutes.

5. Then make a quick pressure release and transfer the cooked chicken in the bowl.

6. Blend the chicken broth mixture with the help of the immersion blender.

7. Add mascarpone cheese and Cheddar cheese. Saute the liquid for 2 minutes on saute mode.

8. Meanwhile, shred the chicken.

9. Add it in the mascarpone mixture and mix it up. Saute the meal for 3 minutes more.

Nutritional info per serve: calories 212, fat 8.9, fiber 0.2, carbs 1.3, protein 29.8

White Chicken Chili

Prep time: 15 minutes | **Cook time:** 15 minutes | **Yield:** 4 servings

Ingredients

1 cup chicken broth

1-pound chicken fillet

1 teaspoon dried oregano

½ cup heavy cream

1 jalapeno, chopped

1 chili pepper, chopped

1 teaspoon cream cheese

Method

1. Put the chicken fillet in the instant pot.

2. Add chicken broth, oregano, heavy cream, jalapeno, and chili powder.

3. Cook the chicken on manual mode (high pressure) for 12 minutes. Make a quick pressure release and shred the chicken with the help of the fork.

4. Then add cream cheese and cook the chili on manual mode (high pressure) for 3 minutes. Allow the natural pressure release for 5 minutes.

Nutritional info per serve: calories 282, fat 14.7, fiber 0.3, carbs 1.2, protein 34.5

Juicy Chicken Breast

Prep time: 10 minutes | **Cook time:** 15 minutes | **Yield:** 2 servings

Ingredients

8 oz chicken breast, skinless, boneless

1 cup of water

¼ cup butter

1 teaspoon chili flakes

1 teaspoon olive oil

Method

1. Heat up olive oil on saute mode for 2 minutes.

2. Then add the chicken breast and cook it for 3 minutes from each side.

3. Add water, butter, and chili flakes.

4. Close and seal the lid and cook the chicken for 10 minutes on High pressure.

5.   Then make a quick pressure release and open the lid.

6.   Slice the cooked chicken breast and sprinkle it with liquid from the instant pot.

Nutritional info per serve: calories 353, fat 28.2, fiber 0, carbs 0.1, protein 24.3

Chicken in Gravy

Prep time: 10 minutes | **Cook time:** 15 minutes | **Yield:** 4 servings

Ingredients

¼ cup broccoli, chopped

2 oz celery stalk, chopped

¼ cup daikon, chopped

1 cup of water

4 chicken thighs

1 teaspoon salt

1 tablespoon coconut cream

Method

1.   Put all ingredients in the instant pot and close the lid.

2.   Cook the mixture for 15 minutes on manual mode (high pressure).

3.   Then make a quick pressure release and open the lid.

4.   Remove the chicken from the liquid.

5.   Blend the liquid with the help of the immersion blender.

6.   Then return the chicken thighs back in the blended sauce and saute the meal for 5 minutes.

Nutritional info per serve: calories 293, fat 11.8, fiber 0.7, carbs 1.5, protein 42.8

Mustard Chicken Breast

Prep time: 10 minutes | **Cook time:** 15 minutes | **Yield:** 2 servings

Ingredients

10 oz chicken breast, boneless

1 tablespoon sunflower oil

2 teaspoons mustard

1 cup of water

Method

1.   Pour water in the instant pot and insert the steamer rack.

2.   In the shallow bowl, mix up sunflower oil and mustard.

3.   Rub the chicken breast with mustard mixture and wrap in the foil.

4.   Put the wrapped chicken on the steamer rack and close the lid.

5.   Cook the meal in manual mode for 15 minutes. Make a quick pressure release.

Nutritional info per serve: calories 239, fat 11.5, fiber 0.5, carbs 1.2, protein 30.9

Butter Chicken

Prep time: 10 minutes | **Cook time:** 20 minutes | **Yield:** 2 servings

Ingredients

8 oz chicken fillet, sliced

1 tomato, chopped

2 tablespoons mascarpone

1 teaspoon coconut oil

1 teaspoon ground paprika

½ teaspoon ground turmeric

1 tablespoon butter

Method

1. Rub the chicken fillet with ground paprika, ground turmeric, and paprika.
2. Put the sliced chicken in the instant pot.
3. Add tomato, mascarpone, coconut oil, and butter.
4. Close the lid and cook the meal on saute mode for 20 minutes.
5. Stir it every 5 minutes to avoid burning.

Nutritional info per serve: calories 323, fat 18.7, fiber 0.9, carbs 2.6, protein 35.1

Parmesan Chicken Fillets

Prep time: 15 minutes | **Cook time:** 13 minutes | **Yield:** 2 servings

Ingredients

1 tomato, sliced
8 oz chicken fillets
2 oz Parmesan, sliced
1 teaspoon butter
4 tablespoons water
1 cup water, for cooking

Method

1. Pour water and insert the steamer rack in the instant pot.
2. Then grease the baking mold with butter.
3. Slice the chicken fillets into halves and put them in the mold.
4. Sprinkle the chicken with water and top with tomato and Parmesan.
5. Cover the baking mold with foil and place it on the rack.
6. Close and seal the lid.

7. Cook the meal in manual mode for 13 minutes. Then allow the natural pressure release for 10 minutes.

Nutritional info per serve: calories 329, fat 16.4, fiber 0.4, carbs 2.2, protein 42.2

Chicken Alfredo

Prep time: 15 minutes | **Cook time:** 10 minutes | **Yield:** 4 servings

Ingredients

½ cup cremini mushrooms, sliced
¼ cup leek, chopped
1 tablespoon sesame oil
1 teaspoon chili flakes
1 cup heavy cream
1-pound chicken fillet, chopped
1 teaspoon Italian seasonings
1 tablespoon cream cheese

Method

1. Brush the instant pot boil with sesame oil from inside.
2. Put the chicken in the instant pot in one layer.
3. Then top it with mushrooms and leek.
4. Sprinkle the ingredients with chili flakes, heavy cream, Italian seasonings, and cream cheese.
5. Close and seal the lid.
6. Cook the meal on manual mode (high pressure) for 10 minutes.
7. When the time is finished, allow the natural pressure release for 10 minutes.

Nutritional info per serve: calories 367, fat 24.2, fiber 0.2, carbs 2.2, protein 33.9

Paprika Chicken Wings

Prep time: 10 minutes | **Cook time:** 13 minutes | **Yield:** 4 servings

Ingredients

1-pound chicken wings, boneless

1 teaspoon ground paprika

1 teaspoon avocado oil

¼ teaspoon minced garlic

¾ cup beef broth

Method

1.   Pour the avocado oil in the instant pot.

2.   Rub the chicken wings with ground paprika and minced garlic and put them in the instant pot.

3.   Cook the chicken on saute mode for 4 minutes from each side.

4.   Then add beef broth and close the lid.

5.   Saute the meal for 5 minutes more.

Nutritional info per serve: calories 226, fat 8.9, fiber 0.3, carbs 0.6, protein 33.8

Cordon Bleu

Prep time: 20 minutes | **Cook time:** 7 minutes | **Yield:** 4 servings

Ingredients

1 cup coconut shred

4 deli ham slices

1-pound chicken breast, skinless, boneless

4 tablespoons butter, melted

1 teaspoon ground black pepper

4 Cheddar cheese slices

1 cup beef broth

Method

1.   Cut the chicken breast into 4 fillets and beat them gently.

2.   Then place the ham on the chicken fillets, add Cheddar cheese slices and roll them.

3.   Mix up ground black pepper and melted butter.

4.   Then dip the rolled chicken in the melted butter and coat in the coconut shred.

5.   Pour beef broth and insert the steamer rack in the instant pot.

6.   Put the chicken on the steamer rack and close the lid.

7.   Cook the meal on manual mode (high pressure) for 7 minutes.

8.   Then allow the natural pressure release for 10 minutes.

Nutritional info per serve: calories 601, fat 46.4, fiber 4.5, carbs 10, protein 37.1

Herbed Whole Chicken

Prep time: 20 minutes | **Cook time:** 25 minutes | **Yield:** 4 servings

Ingredients

1 ½ pound whole chicken

1 tablespoon poultry seasoning

2 tablespoons avocado oil

2 cups of water

Method

1.   Pour water in the instant pot.

2.   Then rub the chicken with poultry seasonings and avocado oil.

3.   Put the chicken in the instant pot. Close and seal the lid.

4.   Cook the meal in manual mode for 25 minutes.

5.   When the time is finished, allow the natural pressure release for 10 minutes.

Nutritional info per serve: calories 335, fat 13.6, fiber 0.4, carbs 1, protein 49.4

Chicken Pasta

Prep time: 10 minutes | **Cook time:** 20 minutes | **Yield:** 4 servings

Ingredients

¼ cup Monterey Jack cheese, shredded

1 tablespoon mascarpone cheese

½ cup coconut cream

1 teaspoon ground black pepper

½ teaspoon salt

1-pound chicken fillet, sliced

1 teaspoon olive oil

Method

1.   Sprinkle the chicken fillet with ground black pepper and salt.

2.   Then put it in the instant pot, add olive oil and cook on saute mode for 10 minutes.

3.   Stir the chicken and add coconut cream and mascarpone cheese. Mix up well.

4.   Add shredded cheese and close the lid.

5.   Saute the chicken pasta for 10 minutes on saute mode.

6.   Stir the cooked chicken pasta well before serving.

Nutritional info per serve: calories 329, fat 19.4, fiber 0.8, carbs 2.2, protein 35.7

Fiesta Chicken

Prep time: 20 minutes | **Cook time:** 15 minutes | **Yield:** 4 servings

Ingredients

1 cup cauliflower, shredded

1 teaspoon taco seasonings

¼ cup bell pepper, chopped

1 tomato, chopped

1 cup chicken broth

½ teaspoon chili flakes

1 tablespoon butter

1-pound chicken thighs, skinless, boneless, chopped

Method

1.   Melt the butter in the instant pot on saute mode.

2.   After this, add bell pepper, tomato, and cauliflower.

3.   Sprinkle the vegetables with taco seasonings and cook them for 10 minutes on saute mode.

4.   After this, add chicken thighs, chili flakes, and chicken broth.

5.   Close and seal the lid and cook the meal on manual mode (high pressure) for 15 minutes.

6.   Allow the natural pressure release for 10 minutes.

Nutritional info per serve: calories 265, fat 11.7, fiber 3.2, carbs 0.9, protein 34.8

Pulled Chicken

Prep time: 10 minutes | **Cook time:** 12 minutes | **Yield:** 2 servings

Ingredients

¼ teaspoon smoked paprika

½ teaspoon ground cumin

3 tablespoons sugar-free ketchup

1 cup of water

1 teaspoon Erythritol

10 oz chicken fillet

Method

1.   Put all the ingredients in the instant pot. Close and seal the lid.

2.   Cook the meal on Manual (high pressure) for 12 minutes.

3.   Then make a quick pressure release and open the lid.

4.   Shred the chicken with the help of 2 forks and transfer in the serving bowls.

5.   Add ½ part of the remaining liquid from the instant pot.

Nutritional info per serve: calories 280, fat 10.7, fiber 0.2, carbs 7.4, protein 41.1

Chicken Masala

Prep time: 10 minutes | **Cook time:** 17 minutes | **Yield:** 3 servings

Ingredients

12 oz chicken fillet

1 tablespoon masala spices

1 tablespoon avocado oil

3 tablespoons organic almond milk

Method

1.   Heat up avocado oil in the instant pot on saute mode for 2 minutes.

2.   Meanwhile, chop the chicken fillet roughly and mix it up with masala spices.

3.   Add almond milk and transfer the chicken in the instant pot.

4.   Cook the chicken bites on saute mode for 15 minutes. Stir the meal occasionally.

Nutritional info per serve: calories 211, fat 8.6, fiber 0.2, carbs 6.2, protein 25.4

Sesame Chicken

Prep time: 15 minutes | **Cook time:** 12 minutes | **Yield:** 2 servings

Ingredients

½ teaspoon of five spices

½ teaspoon sesame seeds

½ cup broccoli, chopped

6 oz chicken fillet, sliced

½ cup chicken broth

1 teaspoon coconut aminos

1 tablespoon avocado oil

Method

1.   In the mixing bowl, mix up avocado oil, coconut aminos, and sesame seeds.

2.   Add five spices.

3.   After this, mix up sliced chicken fillet and coconut aminos mixture.

4.   Put the chicken in the instant pot. Add chicken broth and broccoli.

5.   Close and seal the lid.

6.   Cook the meal on manual mode (high pressure) for 12 minutes. Make a quick pressure release.

Nutritional info per serve: calories 195, fat 8, fiber 1, carbs 2.8, protein 26.7

Chicken Curry with Cilantro

Prep time: 15 minutes | **Cook time:** 12 minutes | **Yield:** 4 servings

Ingredients

1 eggplant, chopped

¼ cup fresh cilantro, chopped

1 teaspoon curry powder

1 cup coconut cream

1 teaspoon coconut oil

1-pound chicken breast, skinless, boneless, cubed

Method

1. Put the coconut oil and chicken breast in the instant pot.

2. Saute the ingredients on saute mode for 5 minutes.

3. Then stir well and add cilantro, eggplant, coconut cream, and curry powder.

4. Close and seal the lid.

5. Cook the meal on manual mode (high pressure) for 7 minutes.

6. Make a quick pressure release and transfer the cooked chicken in the serving bowls.

Nutritional info per serve: calories 308, fat 18.6, fiber 5.6, carbs 10.4, protein 26.6

Tender Chicken Thighs

Prep time: 10 minutes | **Cook time:** 16 minutes | **Yield:** 4 servings

Ingredients

1 teaspoon dried sage

1 teaspoon ground turmeric

2 teaspoons avocado oil

4 chicken thighs, skinless

1 cup of water

1 teaspoon sesame oil

Method

1. Rub the chicken thighs with dried sage, ground turmeric, sesame oil, and avocado oil.

2. Then pour water in the instant pot and insert the steamer rack.

3. Place the chicken thighs on the rack and close the lid.

4. Cook the meal on manual (high pressure) for 16 minutes.

5. Then make a quick pressure release and open the lid.

6. Let the cooked chicken thighs cool for 10 minutes before serving.

Nutritional info per serve: calories 293, fat 12.3, fiber 0.3, carbs 0.6, protein 42.3

Chicken Jalapenos Roll

Prep time: 15 minutes | **Cook time:** 20 minutes | **Yield:** 4 servings

Ingredients

16 oz chicken fillet

2 jalapenos, trimmed, seeded

1 tablespoon olive oil

1 teaspoon Italian seasoning

1 teaspoon ground paprika

½ teaspoon salt

2 Cheddar cheese slices

1 cup water, for cooking

Method

1. Beat the chicken fillet with the help of the kitchen hammer.

2. Then sprinkle it with Italian seasonings, ground paprika, and salt.

3. After this, put the cheese on the fillet. Add jalapenos and roll the chicken fillet into a roll.

4. Brush it with the help of the olive oil and put it in the baking pan.

5. Pour water and insert the steamer rack in the instant pot.

6. Put the baking pan with chicken on the steamer rack. Close and seal the lid.

7. Cook the meal on manual (high pressure) for 20 minutes. Make a quick pressure release.

Nutritional info per serve: calories 309, fat 17, fiber 0.4, carbs 1, protein 36.5

Chicken Nuggets

Prep time: 10 minutes | **Cook time:** 9 minutes | **Yield:** 5 servings

Ingredients

8 oz chicken fillet

1 teaspoon ground turmeric

½ teaspoon ground coriander

½ cup almond flour

2 eggs, beaten

½ cup butter

Method

1. Chop the chicken fillet roughly into the medium size pieces.

2. In the mixing bowl, mix up ground turmeric, ground coriander, and almond flour.

3. Then dip the chicken pieces in the beaten egg and coat in the almond flour mixture.

4. Toss the butter in the instant pot and melt it on saute mode for 4 minutes.

5. Then put the coated chicken in the hot butter and cook for 5 minutes or until the nuggets are golden brown.

Nutritional info per serve: calories 343, fat 28.9, fiber 1.3, carbs 2.8, protein 18

Fajita Strips

Prep time: 10 minutes | **Cook time:** 25 minutes | **Yield:** 4 servings

Ingredients

1 bell pepper, cut into strips

2 oz scallions, chopped

1 teaspoon Fajita seasonings

15 oz chicken fillet, cut into strips

1 teaspoon coconut oil

½ teaspoon ginger paste

Method

1. Heat up coconut oil on saute mode for 3 minutes.

2. Add scallions and bell pepper strips.

3. Saute them for 5 minutes.

4. After this, add Fajita seasonings, chicken strips, and ginger paste.

5. Close the lid and cook the meal for 15 minutes. Stir the chicken from time to time during cooking.

Nutritional info per serve: calories 229, fat 9.1, fiber 0.8, carbs 4, protein 31.3

Thyme Chicken Gizzards

Prep time: 15 minutes | **Cook time:** 25 minutes | **Yield:** 4 servings

Ingredients

1-pound chicken gizzards, chopped

1 cup of water

1 teaspoon dried thyme

1 tablespoon butter

1 teaspoon salt

½ teaspoon peppercorns

Method

1.   Put all ingredients in the instant pot.

2.   Close and seal the lid.

3.   Cook the chicken gizzards on manual mode (high pressure) for 25 minutes.

4.   Allow the natural pressure release for 15 minutes before opening the lid.

Nutritional info per serve: calories 50, fat 3.4, fiber 0.2, carbs 0.3, protein 4.5

Greek Burger

Prep time: 15 minutes | **Cook time:** 20 minutes | **Yield:** 2 servings

Ingredients

1 cup ground chicken

1 tablespoon lemon juice

2 tablespoons coconut flour

½ teaspoon minced garlic

½ teaspoon dried parsley

1 cup water, for cooking

Method

1.   In the mixing bowl, mix up ground chicken, lemon juice, coconut flour, minced garlic, and dried parsley.

2.   Make 2 burgers and place them in the baking pan.

3.   Pour water and insert the steamer rack in the instant pot.

4.   Then place the pan with burgers on the steamer. Close and seal the lid.

5.   Cook the meal on manual mode (high pressure) for 20 minutes. Allow the natural pressure release for 10 minutes.

Nutritional info per serve: calories 173, fat 6.5, fiber 3.1, carbs 5.1, protein 21.9

Dijon Turkey Meatballs

Prep time: 15 minutes | **Cook time:** 14 minutes | **Yield:** 4 servings

Ingredients

14 oz ground turkey

1 tablespoon Dijon mustard

½ cup coconut flour

1 teaspoon onion powder

1 teaspoon salt

½ cup chicken broth

1 tablespoon avocado oil

Method

1.   In the mixing bowl, mix up ground turkey, Dijon mustard, coconut flour, onion powder, and salt.

2.   Make the meatballs with the help of the fingertips.

3.   Then pour avocado oil in the instant pot and heat it up for1 minute.

4. Add the meatballs and cook them for 2 minutes from each side.

5. Then add chicken broth. Close and seal the lid.

6. Cook the meatballs for 10 minutes. Make a quick pressure release.

Nutritional info per serve: calories 268, fat 13.2, fiber 6.3, carbs 11, protein 30

Tender Turkey Tetrazzini

Prep time: 15 minutes | **Cook time:** 20 minutes | **Yield:** 4 servings

Ingredients

14 oz turkey, breast, cooked, shredded

½ cup mushrooms, sliced

2 oz Parmesan, grated

1 cup spaghetti squash, chopped, cooked

2 tablespoons butter, melted

½ cup heavy cream

½ cup Mozzarella, shredded

½ cup of water

Method

1. Put shredded turkey, mushrooms, Parmesan, and spaghetti squash in the instant pot. Mix up well.

2. In the mixing bowl, mix up butter, heavy cream, Mozzarella, and water.

3. Pour the liquid over the turkey.

4. Close and seal the lid.

5. Cook the meal on manual mode (high pressure) for 20 minutes. Allow the natural pressure release for 10 minutes.

Nutritional info per serve: calories 337, fat 20.1, fiber 0.1, carbs 3.1, protein 35.4

Smoky Chicken Breast

Prep time: 10 minutes | **Cook time:** 75 minutes | **Yield:** 4 servings

Ingredients

1-pound chicken breast, skinless, boneless

1 tablespoon Keto ketchup

1 teaspoon Erythritol

1 teaspoon allspices

1 cup chicken broth

Method

1. Put all ingredients in the instant pot.

2. Close the lid and cook the ingredients on Meat/Stew mode for 75 minutes.

3. When the cooking time is finished, open the lid and shred the chicken breast.

4. Stir the meal well before serving.

Nutritional info per serve: calories 144, fat 3.2, fiber 0.1, carbs 2.8, protein 25.4

Cheese Chicken Kofte

Prep time: 10 minutes | **Cook time:** 10 minutes | **Yield:** 4 servings

Ingredients

1 ½ cup ground chicken

1 teaspoon chili flakes

1 teaspoon garlic powder

½ cup Cheddar cheese, shredded

1 egg, beaten

3 tablespoons coconut flour

1 tablespoon coconut oil

Method

1. In the mixing bowl, mix up ground chicken, chili flakes, garlic powder, shredded cheese, egg, and coconut flour.

2. Then make the small meatballs and press them gently with the help of the hand palm.

3. Heat up coconut oil on saute mode for 2 minutes.

4. Then put the chicken kofte inside the instant pot in one layer and cook them for 4 minutes from each side.

Nutritional info per serve: calories 227, fat 13.6, fiber 2.3, carbs 4.5, protein 21

Poblano Chicken Strips

Prep time: 10 minutes | **Cook time:** 29 minutes | **Yield:** 4 servings

Ingredients

2 Poblano peppers, sliced

16 oz chicken fillet

½ teaspoon salt

½ cup coconut cream

1 tablespoon butter

½ teaspoon chili powder

Method

1. Heat up the butter on saute mode for 3 minutes.

2. Add Poblano and cook them for 3 minutes.

3. Meanwhile, cut the chicken fillet into the strips and sprinkle with salt and chili powder.

4. Add the chicken strips to the instant pot.

5. Then add coconut cream and close the lid.

6. Cook the meal on saute mode for 20 minutes.

Nutritional info per serve: calories 320, fat 18.5, fiber 1.1, carbs 4, protein 34

Chicken Lombardy

Prep time: 15 minutes | **Cook time:** 30 minutes | **Yield:** 4 servings

Ingredients

4 chicken thighs

1 oz butter

½ teaspoon garam masala

¼ cup apple cider vinegar

2 tablespoons coconut flour

3 oz Parmesan, grated

½ cup of water

1 oz Mozzarella cheese, shredded

Method

1. Heat up butter on saute mode.

2. When the butter is melted, add chicken thighs and sprinkle them with garam masala. Cook them for 3 minutes from each side.

3. After this, add apple cider vinegar, coconut flour, and ½ cup water.

4. Close and seal the lid and cook the chicken on manual (high pressure) for 15 minutes.

5. Allow the natural pressure release for 10 minutes.

6. Then top the chicken with all cheese and saute for 5 minutes more.

Nutritional info per serve: calories 435, fat 22.7, fiber 1.5, carbs 3.7, protein 51.6

Chicken with Pizza Stuffing

Prep time: 20 minutes | **Cook time:** 12 minutes | **Yield:** 4 servings

Ingredients

12 oz chicken fillet

3 oz ground sausages

½ bell pepper, chopped

½ teaspoon chili flakes

¼ cup Cheddar cheese, shredded

½ tomato, chopped

1 teaspoon Italian seasonings

1 cup water, for cooking

Method

1.   In the mixing bowl, mix up ground sausages, bell pepper, chili flakes, Cheddar cheese, tomato, and Italian seasonings.

2.   Then make the cut (pocket) in the chicken fillet and fill it with ground sausages mixture.

3.   Wrap the chicken in the foil and place it on the steamer rack.

4.   Pour water and transfer the steamer rack in the instant pot.

5.   Cook the meal on manual mode (high pressure) for 22 minutes. Allow the natural pressure release for 10 minutes.

Nutritional info per serve: calories 272, fat 15.1, fiber 0.3, carbs 1.7, protein 30.7

Philadelphia Stuffed Chicken Breast

Prep time: 10 minutes | **Cook time:** 16 minutes | **Yield:** 5 servings

Ingredients

1-pound chicken breast, skinless, boneless

2 tablespoons cream cheese

1 tablespoon chives, chopped

½ teaspoon minced garlic

½ teaspoon salt

1 tablespoon avocado oil

1 cup water, for cooking

Method

1.   Make the cut in the shape of the pocket in the chicken breast. Rub the chicken with salt.

2.   After this, in the mixing bowl, mix up cream cheese, chives, and minced garlic.

3.   Rub the chicken breast with salt and fill with the cream cheese.

4.   Then secure the "chicken pocket" with the help of the toothpicks.

5.   Pour water and insert the steamer rack in the instant pot.

6.   Then put the chicken breast in the baking pan and transfer it on the rack.

7.   Cook the meal on manual mode (high pressure) for 25 minutes. Allow the natural pressure release for 10 minutes.

Nutritional info per serve: calories 122, fat 4, fiber 0.2, carbs 0.4, protein 19.6

Chicken Fingers

Prep time: 10 minutes | **Cook time:** 7 minutes | **Yield:** 4 servings

Ingredients

2 eggs, beaten

1 tablespoon coconut cream

½ teaspoon ground paprika

½ teaspoon ground turmeric

½ teaspoon salt

½ cup almond flour

1-pound chicken fillet

1 tablespoon coconut oil

Method

1. Cut the chicken fillet on the strips and sprinkle with salt, ground paprika, and ground turmeric.

2. In the mixing bowl, mix up coconut cream and eggs.

3. Then dip the chicken strips in the egg mixture. After this, coat the chicken in the almond flour.

4. Repeat the steps one more time.

5. Then preheat the coconut oil on saute mode for 2 minutes and put the chicken strips inside in one layer.

6. Cook the chicken strips on saute mode for 3 minutes from each side.

Nutritional info per serve: calories 371, fat 21.6, fiber 1.7, carbs 3.7, protein 38.7

Pancetta Wings

Prep time: 15 minutes | **Cook time:** 7 minutes | **Yield:** 4 servings

Ingredients

4 chicken wings

2 oz pancetta, sliced

1 teaspoon ground black pepper

½ teaspoon salt

1 cup water, for cooking

Method

1. Put the sliced pancetta in the baking pan in one layer.

2. Then sprinkle the chicken wings with ground black pepper and salt and place them over the pancetta.

3. Cover the chicken with foil.

4. After this, pour water and insert the steamer rack in the instant pot.

5. Put the baking pan with chicken on the rack. Close and seal the lid.

6. Cook the chicken wings on manual mode (high pressure) for 7 minutes. Then allow the natural pressure release for 10 minutes.

Nutritional info per serve: calories 177, fat 12.6, fiber 0.1, carbs 0.5, protein 14.4

Provolone Stuffed Chicken

Prep time: 15 minutes | **Cook time:** 20 minutes | **Yield:** 4 servings

Ingredients

12 oz chicken fillet

4 oz provolone cheese, sliced

1 tablespoon cream cheese

½ teaspoon dried cilantro

½ teaspoon smoked paprika

1 cup water, for cooking

Method

1. Beat the chicken fillet well and rub it with dried cilantro and smoked paprika.

2. Then spread it with cream cheese and top with Provolone cheese.

3. Roll the chicken fillet into the roll and wrap in the foil.

4. Pour water and insert the rack in the instant pot.

5. Place the chicken roll on the rack. Close and seal the lid.

6. Cook it on manual mode (high pressure) for 20 minutes.

7. Make a quick pressure release and slice the chicken roll into the servings.

Nutritional info per serve: calories 271, fat 14.8, fiber 0.1, carbs 0.8, protein 32.1

FISH AND SEAFOOD

Cioppino Stew

Prep time: 10 minutes | **Cook time:** 2 minutes | **Yield:** 4 servings

Ingredients

7 oz scallops

4 oz shrimps, peeled

1 tablespoon Italian seasonings

½ teaspoon minced garlic

1 cup beef broth

1 teaspoon tomato paste

Method

1.   Put all ingredients in the instant pot and mix up gently with the help of the spoon.

2.   Close and seal the lid.

3.   Cook the stew on manual mode (high pressure) for 2 minutes. Allow the natural pressure release for 5 minutes.

Nutritional info per serve: calories 99, fat 2.3, fiber 0.1, carbs 2.6, protein 16.1

Bang Bang Shrimps

Prep time: 10 minutes | **Cook time:** 5 minutes | **Yield:** 4 servings

Ingredients

1-pound shrimps, peeled

½ cup almond flour

1 tablespoon olive oil

½ teaspoon salt

1 tablespoon mascarpone cheese

Method

1.   In the mixing bowl, mix up salt and almond flour.

2.   Then dip the shrimps in the mascarpone cheese and coat in the almond flour.

3.   Heat up the olive oil in the instant pot on saute mode for 2 minutes.

4.   Put the coated shrimps in the instant pot and cook them on saute mode for 1.5 minutes from each side.

Nutritional info per serve: calories 256, fat 12.6, fiber 1.5, carbs .4.8, protein 29.3

Apple Cider Vinegar Mussels

Prep time: 10 minutes | **Cook time:** 5 minutes | **Yield:** 6 servings

Ingredients

18 oz mussels, fresh

1 cup apple cider vinegar

1 teaspoon coconut oil, melted

¼ cup of water

1 teaspoon minced garlic

Method

1.   Pour water and apple cider vinegar in the instant pot.

2.   Then insert the steamer rack.

3.   Put the mussels in the instant pot mold.

4.   Sprinkle them with coconut oil and minced garlic.

5.   Close and seal the lid.

6.   Cook the seafood on manual (high pressure) for 3 minutes. Make a quick pressure release.

7. If the mussels are not opened, cook them 2 minutes extra.

Nutritional info per serve: calories 89, fat 2.7, fiber 0, carbs 3.7, protein 10.2

Thyme Lobster Tails

Prep time: 10 minutes | **Cook time:** 4 minutes | **Yield:** 4 servings

Ingredients

4 lobster tails

1 tablespoon butter, softened

1 teaspoon dried thyme

1 cup of water

Method

1. Pour water and insert the steamer rack in the instant pot.

2. Put the lobster tails on the rack and close the lid.

3. Cook the meal on manual mode (high pressure) for 4 minutes. Make a quick pressure release.

4. After this, mix up butter and dried thyme.

5. Peel the lobsters and rub them with thyme butter.

Nutritional info per serve: calories 126, fat 2.9, fiber 0.1, carbs 0.2, protein 24.1

Blackened Salmon

Prep time: 10 minutes | **Cook time:** 4 minutes | **Yield:** 3 servings

Ingredients

1-pound salmon fillet

1 teaspoon ground black pepper

½ teaspoon salt

1 teaspoon ground turmeric

1 teaspoon lemon juice

1 cup of water

Method

1. In the shallow bowl, mix up salt, ground black pepper, and ground turmeric.

2. Sprinkle the salmon fillet with lemon juice and rub with the spice mixture.

3. Then pour water in the instant pot and insert the steamer rack.

4. Wrap the salmon fillet in the foil and place it on the rack.

5. Close and seal the lid.

6. Cook the fish on manual mode (high pressure) for 4 minutes.

7. Make a quick pressure release and cut the fish on servings.

Nutritional info per serve: calories 205, fat 9.4, fiber 0.4, carbs 1, protein 29.5

Shrimp Curry with Coconut Milk

Prep time: 10 minutes | **Cook time:** 4 minutes | **Yield:** 5 servings

Ingredients

15 oz shrimps, peeled

1 teaspoon chili powder

1 teaspoon garam masala

1 cup of coconut milk

1 teaspoon olive oil

½ teaspoon minced garlic

Method

1.   Heat up the instant pot on saute mode for 2 minutes.

2.   Then add olive oil. Cook the ingredients for 1 minute.

3.   Add shrimps and sprinkle them with chili powder, garam masala, minced garlic, and coconut milk.

4.   Carefully stir the ingredients and close the lid.

5.   Cook the shrimp curry on manual mode for 1 minute. Make a quick pressure release.

Nutritional info per serve: calories 222, fat 13.9, fiber 1.3, carbs 4.4, protein 20.6

Alaskan Crab Legs

Prep time: 10 minutes | **Cook time:** 4 minutes | **Yield:** 4 servings

Ingredients

1-pound Alaskan crab legs

1 tablespoon butter

¼ teaspoon dried cilantro

1 cup of water

Method

1.   Pour water in the instant pot.

2.   Add dried cilantro and crab legs.

3.   Cook the on manual mode (high pressure) for 4 minutes.

4.   Then make a quick pressure release.

5.   Peel the crab legs and sprinkle them with butter.

Nutritional info per serve: calories 78, fat 3.3, fiber 0.1, carbs 0.3, protein 12

Cajun Cod

Prep time: 10 minutes | **Cook time:** 4 minutes | **Yield:** 2 servings

Ingredients

10 oz cod fillet

1 tablespoon olive oil

1 teaspoon Cajun seasonings

2 tablespoons coconut aminos

Method

1.   Sprinkle the cod fillet with coconut aminos and Cajun seasonings.

2.   Then heat up olive oil in the instant pot on saute mode.

3.   Add the spiced cod fillet and cook it for 4 minutes from each side.

4.   Then cut it into halves and sprinkle with the oily liquid from the instant pot.

Nutritional info per serve: calories 189, fat 8.3, fiber 0, carbs 3, protein 25.3

Louisiana Gumbo

Prep time: 10 minutes | **Cook time:** 4 minutes | **Yield:** 6 servings

Ingredients

1-pound shrimps

¼ cup celery stalk, chopped

1 chili pepper, chopped

¼ cup okra, chopped

1 tablespoon coconut oil

2 cups chicken broth

1 teaspoon tomato paste

Method

1. Put all ingredients in the instant pot and stir until you get a light red color.

2. Then close and seal the lid.

3. Cook the meal on manual mode (high pressure) for 4 minutes.

4. When the time is finished, allow the natural pressure release for 10 minutes.

Nutritional info per serve: calories 126, fat 4, fiber 0.3, carbs 2.1, protein 19

Lemon Salmon

Prep time: 10 minutes | **Cook time:** 4 minutes | **Yield:** 4 servings

Ingredients

1-pound salmon fillet

1 tablespoon butter, melted

2 tablespoons lemon juice

1 teaspoon dried dill

1 cup of water

Method

1. Cut the salmon fillet on 4 servings.

2. Line the instant pot baking pan with foil and put the salmon fillets inside in one layer.

3. Then sprinkle the fish with dried dill, lemon juice, and butter.

4. Pour water in the instant pot and insert the rack.

5. Place the baking pan with salmon on the rack and close the lid.

6. Cook the meal on manual mode (high pressure) for 4 minutes. Allow the natural pressure release for 5 minutes and remove the fish from the instant pot.

Nutritional info per serve: calories 178, fat 10, fiber 0.1, carbs 0.3, protein 22.1

Boiled Crawfish

Prep time: 5 minutes | **Cook time:** 5 minutes | **Yield:** 4 servings

Ingredients

16 oz crawfish

1 teaspoon old bay seasonings

1 cup of water

Method

1. Pour water in the instant pot bowl.

2. Add old bay seasonings and crawfish.

3. Close and seal the lid and cook the seafood on manual mode (high pressure) for 5 minutes.

4. Then make a quick pressure release and transfer the cooked crawfish in the plate.

Nutritional info per serve: calories 99, fat 1.5, fiber 0, carbs 0, protein 19.9

Spinach Tuna Cakes

Prep time: 15 minutes | **Cook time:** 8 minutes | **Yield:** 4 servings

Ingredients

10 oz tuna, grinded

1 cup spinach

1 egg, beaten

1 teaspoon ground coriander

2 tablespoon coconut flakes

1 tablespoon avocado oil

Method

1. Blend the spinach in the blender until smooth.

2. Then transfer it in the mixing bowl and add grinded tuna, egg, and ground coriander.

3. Add coconut flakes and stir the mass with the help of the spoon.

4. Heat up avocado oil in the instant pot on saute mode for 2 minutes.

5. Then make the medium size cakes from the tuna mixture and place them in the hot oil.

6. Cook the tuna cakes on saute mode for 3 minutes.

7. Then flip the on another side and cook for 3 minutes more or until they are light brown.

Nutritional info per serve: calories 163, fat 8.1, fiber 0.6, carbs 0.9, protein 20.5

Spicy Cod

Prep time: 10 minutes | **Cook time:** 10 minutes | **Yield:** 2 servings

Ingredients

2 cod fillet

¼ teaspoon chili powder

½ teaspoon cayenne pepper

½ teaspoon dried oregano

1 tablespoon lime juice

2 tablespoons avocado oil

Method

1. Rub the cod fillets with chili powder, cayenne pepper, dried oregano, and sprinkle with lime juice.

2. Then pour the avocado oil in the instant pot and heat it up on saute mode for 2 minutes.

3. Put the cod fillets in the hot oil and cook for 5 minutes.

4. Then flip the fish on another side and cook for 5 minutes more.

Nutritional info per serve: calories 114, fat 3, fiber 1, carbs 2, protein 20.3

Pulpo Gallego

Prep time: 10 minutes | **Cook time:** 15 minutes | **Yield:** 4 servings

Ingredients

1-pound octopus, rinsed

1 garlic clove, diced

1 teaspoon salt

1 tablespoon avocado oil

1 cup of water

Method

1. Put the octopus in the instant pot.

2. Add avocado oil, salt, and diced garlic. Mix up the ingredients and add water.

3. Close and seal the lid.

4. Cook the meal on manual mode (high pressure) for 15 minutes.

5. Then allow the natural pressure release for 10 minutes.

6. Transfer the cooked octopus on the serving plate.

Nutritional info per serve: calories 192, fat 2.8, fiber 0.2, carbs 5.4, protein 33.9

Chili Haddock

Prep time: 10 minutes | **Cook time:** 5 minutes | **Yield:** 4 servings

Ingredients

1 chili pepper, minced

1-pound haddock, chopped

½ teaspoon ground turmeric

½ cup fish stock

1 cup of water

Method

1.   In the mixing bowl mix up chili pepper, ground turmeric, and fish stock.

2.   Then add chopped haddock and transfer the mixture in the baking mold.

3.   Pour water in the instant pot and insert the trivet.

4.   Place the baking mold with fish on the trivet and close the lid.

5.   Cook the meal on manual (high pressure) for 5 minutes. Make a quick pressure release.

Nutritional info per serve: calories 130, fat 1.1, fiber 0.1, carbs 0.3, protein 28

Clam Chowder

Prep time: 10 minutes | **Cook time:** 4 minutes | **Yield:** 2 servings

Ingredients

5 oz clams

1 oz bacon, chopped

3 oz celery, chopped

½ cup of water

½ cup heavy cream

Method

1.   Cook the bacon on saute mode for 1 minute.

2.   Then add clams, celery, water, and heavy cream.

3.   Close and seal the lid.

4.   Cook the seafood on steam mode (high pressure) for 3 minutes. Make a quick pressure release.

5.   Ladle the clams with the heavy cream mixture in the bowls.

Nutritional info per serve: calories 221, fat 17.2, fiber 1, carbs 10.1, protein 6.6

Italian Style Salmon

Prep time: 10 minutes | **Cook time:** 4 minutes | **Yield:** 2 servings

Ingredients

10 oz salmon fillet

1 teaspoon Italian seasonings

1 cup of water

Method

1.   Pour water and insert the trivet in the instant pot.

2.   Then rub the salmon fillet with Italian seasonings and wrap in the foil.

3.   Place the wrapped fish on the trivet and close the lid.

4.   Cook the meal on manual mode (high pressure) for 4 minutes.

5.   Make a quick pressure release and remove the fish from the foil.

6.   Cut it into servings.

Nutritional info per serve: calories 195, fat 9.5, fiber 0, carbs 0.3, protein 27.5

Butter Clams

Prep time: 10 minutes | **Cook time:** 3 minutes |
Yield: 2 servings

Ingredients

7 oz clams

2 tablespoons butter

1 cup of water

1 teaspoon minced garlic

Method

1. Pour water in the instant pot.
2. Add clams and close the lid.
3. Cook the cams on high pressure for 3 minutes.
4. When the time is over, make a quick pressure release and transfer the hot clams in the bowl.
5. Add butter and minced garlic.
6. Shake the seafood well.

Nutritional info per serve: calories 152, fat 11.7, fiber 0.4, carbs 11.3, protein 0.8

Fish Curry

Prep time: 10 minutes | **Cook time:** 3 minutes |
Yield: 2 servings

Ingredients

8 oz cod fillet, chopped

1 teaspoon curry paste

1 cup organic almond milk

Method

1. Mix up curry paste and almond milk and pour the liquid in the instant pot.
2. Add chopped cod fillet and close the lid.
3. Cook the fish curry on manual mode (high pressure) for 3 minutes.
4. Then make the quick pressure release for 5 minutes.

Nutritional info per serve: calories 138, fat 3.7, fiber 0, carbs 4.7, protein 20.9

Shrimp Skewers

Prep time: 10 minutes | **Cook time:** 2 minutes |
Yield: 4 servings

Ingredients

1 tablespoon lemon juice

1 teaspoon coconut aminos

12 oz shrimps, peeled

1 teaspoon olive oil

1 cup of water

Method

1. Put the shrimps in the mixing bowl.
2. Add lemon juice, coconut aminos, and olive oil.
3. Then string the shrimps on the skewers.
4. Pour water in the instant pot.
5. Then insert the trivet.
6. Put the shrimp skewers on the trivet.
7. Close the lid and cook the seafood on manual mode (high pressure) for 2 minutes.
8. When the time is finished, make a quick pressure release.

Nutritional info per serve: calories 113, fat 2.6, fiber 0, carbs 1.6, protein 19.4

Salmon Cakes

Prep time: 15 minutes | **Cook time:** 10 minutes | **Yield:** 4 servings

Ingredients

1-pound salmon fillet, chopped

1 tablespoon dill, chopped

2 eggs, beaten

½ cup almond flour

1 tablespoon coconut oil

Method

1. Put the chopped salmon, dill, eggs, and almond flour in the food processor.

2. Blend the mixture until it is smooth.

3. Then make the small balls (cakes) from the salmon mixture.

4. After this, heat up the coconut oil on saute mode for 3 minutes.

5. Put the salmon cakes in the instant pot in one layer and cook them on saute mode for 2 minutes from each side or until they are light brown.

Nutritional info per serve: calories 297, fat 19.3, fiber 1.6, carbs 3.6, protein 27.9

Rosemary Catfish Steak

Prep time: 10 minutes | **Cook time:** 20 minutes | **Yield:** 4 servings

Ingredients

16 oz catfish fillet

1 tablespoon dried rosemary

1 teaspoon garlic powder

1 tablespoon avocado oil

1 teaspoon salt

1 cup water, for cooking

Method

1. Cut the catfish fillet into 4 steaks.

2. Then sprinkle them with dried rosemary, garlic powder, avocado oil, and salt.

3. Place the fish steak in the baking mold in one layer.

4. After this, pour water and insert the steamer rack in the instant pot.

5. Put the baking mold with fish on the rack. Close and seal the lid.

6. Cook the meal on manual (high pressure) for 20 minutes. Make a quick pressure release.

Nutritional info per serve: calories 163, fat 9.2, fiber 0.6, carbs 1.2, protein 17.8

Lime Mahi Mahi

Prep time: 10 minutes | **Cook time:** 9 minutes | **Yield:** 4 servings

Ingredients

1-pound mahi-mahi fillet

1 teaspoon lemon zest, grated

1 tablespoon lemon juice

1 tablespoon butter, softened

½ teaspoon salt

1 cup water, for cooking

Method

1. Cut the fish on 4 servings and sprinkle with lemon zest, lemon juice, salt, and rub with softened butter.

2. Then put the fish in the baking pan in one layer.

3. Pour water and insert the steamer rack in the instant pot.

4. Put the mold with fish on the rack. Close and seal the lid.

5. Cook the Mahi Mahi on manual mode (high pressure) for 9 minutes. Make a quick pressure release.

Nutritional info per serve: calories 128, fat 4, fiber 0.1, carbs 0.2, protein 21.5

Pesto Flounder

Prep time: 15 minutes | **Cook time:** 15 minutes | **Yield:** 3 servings

Ingredients

2 tablespoons pesto sauce

½ cup butter

10 oz flounder fillet

1 cup water, for cooking

Method

1. Cut the fish into 3 servings and put in the baking pan.

2. Brush the flounder fillets with pesto sauce. Add butter.

3. Pour water and insert the steamer rack in the instant pot.

4. Put the baking pan with fish on the rack. Close and seal the lid.

5. Cook the meal on manual mode (high pressure) for 15 minutes. Allow the natural pressure release for 10 minutes.

Nutritional info per serve: calories 427, fat 36.5, fiber 0.2, carbs 0.7, protein 24.2

Salmon Caprese

Prep time: 10 minutes | **Cook time:** 15 minutes | **Yield:** 2 servings

Ingredients

10 oz salmon fillet (2 fillets)

4 oz Mozzarella, sliced

4 cherry tomatoes, sliced

1 teaspoon Erythritol

1 teaspoon dried basil

½ teaspoon ground black pepper

1 tablespoon apple cider vinegar

1 tablespoon butter

1 cup water, for cooking

Method

1. Grease the mold with butter and put the salmon inside.

2. Sprinkle the fish with Erythritol, dried basil, ground black pepper, and apple cider vinegar.

3. Then top the salmon with tomatoes and Mozzarella.

4. Pour water and insert the steamer rack in the instant pot.

5. Put the fish on the rack.

6. Close and seal the lid.

7. Cook the meal on manual mode (high pressure0 for 15 minutes. Make a quick pressure release.

Nutritional info per serve: calories 447, fat 25, fiber 3.2, carbs 14.8, protein 45.9

Seafood Zoodle Alfredo

Prep time: 10 minutes | **Cook time:** 10 minutes | **Yield:** 4 servings

Ingredients

2 zucchinis, trimmed

1 cup coconut cream

1 teaspoon butter

1 teaspoon seafood seasonings

6 oz shrimps, peeled

Method

1.   Melt the butter on saute mode and add shrimps.

2.   Sprinkle them with seafood seasonings and saute then for 2 minutes.

3.   After this, spiralizer the zucchini with the help of the spiralizer and add in the shrimps.

4.   Add coconut cream and close the lid. Cook the meal on saute mode for 8 minutes.

Nutritional info per serve: calories 213, fat 16.2, fiber 2.4, carbs 7.3, protein 12.3

Cod with Olives

Prep time: 15 minutes | **Cook time:** 10 minutes | **Yield:** 2 servings

Ingredients

8 oz cod fillet

¼ cup olives, sliced

1 teaspoon olive oil

¼ teaspoon salt

1 cup water, for cooking

Method

1.   Pour water and insert the steamer rack in the instant pot.

2.   Then cut the cod fillet into 2 servings and sprinkle with salt and olive oil.

3.   Then place the fish on the foil and top with the sliced olives. Wrap the fish and transfer it in the steamer rack.

4.   Close and seal the lid. Cook the fish on manual mode (high pressure) for 10 minutes.

5.   Allow the natural pressure release for 5 minutes.

Nutritional info per serve: calories 130, fat 5.1, fiber 0.5, carbs 1.1, protein 20.4

VEGAN

Cauliflower Tikka Masala

Prep time: 10 minutes | **Cook time:** 3 minutes | **Yield:** 6 servings

Ingredients

1-pound cauliflower, chopped

1 teaspoon garam masala

1 tablespoon coconut oil

1 teaspoon ground turmeric

3 oz scallions, chopped

1 cup of coconut milk

¼ cup crushed tomatoes

Method

1. Put all ingredients in the instant pot and mix them well.

2. Then close and seal the lid.

3. Cook the tikka masala for 3 minutes on manual mode (high pressure).

4. Then allow the natural pressure release for 5 minutes.

5. Shake the cooked meal well before serving.

Nutritional info per serve: calories 140, fat 12, fiber 3.6, carbs 8.3, protein 3

Spiced Cauliflower Head

Prep time: 15 minutes | **Cook time:** 17 minutes | **Yield:** 4 servings

Ingredients

13 oz cauliflower head

1 tablespoon avocado oil

1 tablespoon coconut cream

1 teaspoon ground turmeric

1 teaspoon ground paprika

½ teaspoon salt

½ teaspoon ground cumin

1 cup of water

Method

1. Pour water in the instant pot and insert the steamer rack.

2. In the mixing bowl, mix up avocado oil, coconut cream, ground turmeric, paprika, salt, and ground cumin.

3. Carefully brush the cauliflower head with a coconut cream mixture.

4. Sprinkle the remaining coconut cream mixture over the cauliflower.

5. Transfer the vegetable on the steamer rack.

6. Close and seal the lid.

7. Cook the cauliflower on manual mode (high pressure) for 7 minutes.

8. When the time is finished, allow the natural pressure release for 10 minutes.

Nutritional info per serve: calories 41, fat 1.6, fiber 2.9, carbs 6.1, protein 2.1

Parm Zucchini Noodles

Prep time: 10 minutes | **Cook time:** 5 minutes | **Yield:** 2 servings

Ingredients

1 large zucchini

1 garlic clove, diced

1 tablespoon butter

3 oz Parmesan, grated

½ teaspoon chili flakes

Method

1. Trim the zucchini and make the spirals from it with the help of the spiralizer.

2. Then toss the butter in the instant pot and melt it on saute mode.

3. Add garlic and chili flakes and cook the ingredients for 2 minutes.

4. After this, add zucchini spirals and cook them for 2 minutes.

5. Add grated Parmesan and mix up the meal well. Cook it for 1 minute more.

Nutritional info per serve: calories 216, fat 15.2, fiber 1.8, carbs 7.5, protein 15.8

Tempeh Satay

Prep time: 5 minutes | **Cook time:** 4 minutes | **Yield:** 6 servings

Ingredients

15 oz tempeh

1 tablespoon coconut aminos

½ teaspoon harissa

1 tablespoon almond butter

Method

1. Chop the tempeh into cubes.

2. Then put the almond butter and harissa in the instant pot and melt it on saute mode.

3. Add chopped tempeh and coconut aminos.

4. Cook the meal on saute mode for 2 minutes – for 1 minute from each side.

Nutritional info per serve: calories 157, fat 9.2, fiber 0.3, carbs 7.8, protein 13.7

Teriyaki Eggplants

Prep time: 10 minutes | **Cook time:** 6 minutes | **Yield:** 6 servings

Ingredients

3 eggplants, trimmed

2 tablespoons keto teriyaki

2 tablespoons sesame oil

½ teaspoon ground ginger

½ teaspoon sesame seeds

Method

1. Heat up sesame oil in saute mode for 2 minutes.

2. Meanwhile, slice the eggplants and sprinkle them with teriyaki, ground ginger, and sesame seeds.

3. Arrange the eggplant slices in the instant pot bowl in one layer and cook them on saute mode for 2 minutes from each side.

Nutritional info per serve: calories 116, fat 5.2, fiber 9.7, carbs 17.2, protein 3.1

Kale Stir Fry

Prep time: 10 minutes | **Cook time:** 3 minutes | **Yield:** 4 servings

Ingredients

8 oz asparagus, chopped

2 cups kale, chopped

2 bell pepper, chopped

½ teaspoon minced ginger

1 tablespoon avocado oil

1 teaspoon apple cider vinegar

½ cup of water

Method

1.   In the instant pot baking pan, mix up together chopped kale, asparagus, bell pepper, minced ginger, apple cider vinegar, and avocado oil.

2.   Then pour water in the instant pot.

3.   Insert the steamer rack and place the mold with a kale mixture on it.

4.   Close and seal the lid and cook the kale stir fry for 3 minutes on manual mode (high pressure). Make a quick pressure release.

Nutritional info per serve: calories 53, fat 0.7, fiber 2.7, carbs 10.6, protein 2.9

Tofu Quiche

Prep time: 10 minutes | **Cook time:** 8 minutes | **Yield:** 4 servings

Ingredients

8 oz tofu

½ cup mushrooms, chopped, fried

1 teaspoon nutritional yeast

2 tablespoons almond flour

1 teaspoon coconut milk

1 teaspoon dried dill

¼ teaspoon salt

1 cup water, for cooking

Method

1.   Chop tofu and mix it up with mushrooms, nutritional yeast, almond flour, coconut milk, dried dill, and salt.

2.   Then place the mixture in the baking pan and flatten in the shape of the quiche.

3.   Pour water in the instant pot and insert the steamer rack.

4.   Place the quiche on the rack and close the lid.

5.   Cook the meal on manual mode (high pressure) for 8 minutes. Then make a quick pressure release.

Nutritional info per serve: calories 69, fat 4.4, fiber 1.3, carbs 2.6, protein 6.1

Thyme Cabbage

Prep time: 10 minutes | **Cook time:** 5 minutes | **Yield:** 4 servings

Ingredients

1-pound white cabbage

1 teaspoon dried thyme

2 tablespoons butter

1 cup of water

½ teaspoon salt

Method

1.   Cut the white cabbage on medium size petals.

2.   Then sprinkle it with dried thyme, butter, and salt.

3.   Put the cabbage petals in the instant pot pan.

4.   After this, pour water and insert the steamer rack in the instant pot.

5.   Put the pan with cabbage on the rack and close the lid.

6.   Cook the meal on manual mode (high pressure) for 5 minutes. Make a quick pressure release.

Nutritional info per serve: calories 80, fat 5.9, fiber 2.9, carbs 6.7, protein 1.5

Herbed Radish

Prep time: 5 minutes | **Cook time:** 10 minutes | **Yield:** 2 servings

Ingredients

2 cups radish, roughly chopped

2 tablespoons butter

1 teaspoon Italian seasonings

¼ teaspoon dried rosemary

¼ cup of water

Method

1. Put all ingredients in the instant pot and mix them up.

2. Saute the meal for 10 minutes, Stir it with the help of the spatula every 3 minutes.

Nutritional info per serve: calories 128, fat 12.4, fiber 1.9, carbs 4.3, protein 0.9

Jicama Mash

Prep time: 10 minutes | **Cook time:** 8 minutes | **Yield:** 4 servings

Ingredients

1-pound jicama, peeled, chopped

1 tablespoon almond butter

1 tablespoon chives, chopped

½ cup of coconut milk

Method

1. Put all ingredients from the list above in the instant pot.

2. Close and seal the lid.

3. Cook the jicama for 8 minutes on manual mode (high pressure), make quick pressure release.

4. Then transfer the mixture in the blender and blend until smooth.

Nutritional info per serve: calories 137, fat 9.5, fiber 6.6, carbs 12.4, protein 2.4

Spiced Broccoli

Prep time: 10 minutes | **Cook time:** 4 minutes | **Yield:** 4 servings

Ingredients

2 cups broccoli florets

1 tablespoon lemon juice

1 teaspoon lemon zest, grated

½ teaspoon chili powder

1 tablespoon ground paprika

1 cup of water

1 teaspoon olive oil

Method

1. Pour water in the instant pot and insert the rack.

2. Put broccoli, lemon juice, lemon zest, chili powder, ground paprika, and olive oil in the baking pan and shake gently.

3. Then place the pan on the rack.

4. Close and seal the lid.

5. Cook the broccoli for 4 minutes on manual mode (high pressure).

6. Then make a quick pressure release.

Nutritional info per serve: calories 33, fat 1.6, fiber 2, carbs 4.3, protein 1.6

Cauliflower Gnocchi

Prep time: 10 minutes | **Cook time:** 2 minutes | **Yield:** 4 servings

Ingredients

2 cups cauliflower, boiled

1 teaspoon salt

½ cup almond flour

1 tablespoon sesame oil

1 cup of water

Method

1. Mash the cauliflower until you get puree and mix it up with salt, almond flour, and sesame oil.

2. Then make the log from the cauliflower dough and cut it on small pieces.

3. Pour water in the instant pot.

4. Add gnocchi. Close and seal the lid.

5. Cook the meal on manual mode (high pressure) for 2 minutes.

6. Then allow the natural pressure release and open the lid.

7. Remove the cooked gnocchi from the water.

Nutritional info per serve: calories 127, fat 10.1, fiber 2.8, carbs 5.7, protein 4

Chives Mushrooms

Prep time: 10 minutes | **Cook time:** 3 minutes | **Yield:** 2 servings

Ingredients

1 cup cremini mushrooms, sliced

2 tablespoons chives, chopped

1 tablespoon sesame oil

1 teaspoon ranch seasonings

1 cup of water

Method

1. In the mixing bowl, mix up mushrooms, chives, sesame oil, and ranch seasonings.

2. Then pour water and insert the steamer rack in the instant pot.

3. Put the mushroom mixture in the baking pan and transfer it on the steamer rack.

4. Cook the meal on manual mode (high pressure) for 3 minutes.

5. When the time is finished, make a quick pressure release.

Nutritional info per serve: calories 70, fat 6.9, fiber 0.3, carbs 1.6, protein 1

Zucchini Fritters

Prep time: 15 minutes | **Cook time:** 10 minutes | **Yield:** 4 servings

Ingredients

2 large zucchinis, grated

1 teaspoon ground flax meal

1 daikon, diced

1 egg, beaten

1 tablespoon coconut oil

1 teaspoon salt

Method

1. In the mixing bowl, mix up grated zucchini, ground flax meal, daikon, egg, and salt.

2. Make the fritters from the zucchini mixture.

3. After this, melt the coconut oil on saute mode.

4.   Put the zucchini fritters in the hot oil and cook them for 4 minutes from each side or until they are golden brown.

Nutritional info per serve: calories 76, fat 4.9, fiber 2.1, carbs 6.3, protein 3.6

Mashed Turnips

Prep time: 10 minutes | **Cook time:** 5 minutes | **Yield:** 4 servings

Ingredients

2 cups turnips, peeled, chopped

3 cups of water

1 tablespoon coconut milk

1 teaspoon salt

1 oz tempeh, shredded

Method

1.   Put turnips, water, and salt in the instant pot.

2.   Close and seal the lid.

3.   Cook the turnip on manual mode (high pressure) for 5 minutes. Make a quick pressure release.

4.   Then open the lid and transfer the turnip in the blender.

5.   Add tempeh and coconut milk.

6.   Blend the meal until it is smooth.

7.   Transfer the cooked turnips in the serving bowls.

Nutritional info per serve: calories 49, fat 1.7, fiber 1.6, carbs 6.9, protein 2.2

DESSERTS

Pumpkin Pie Spices Cheesecake

Prep time: 10 minutes | **Cook time:** 40 minutes | **Yield:** 8 servings

Ingredients

3 tablespoons almond flour

1 tablespoon butter, softened

3 tablespoons Erythritol

1 cup cream cheese

1 egg, beaten

¼ cup of coconut milk

1 teaspoon pumpkin pie spices

1 cup water, for cooking

Method

1.   In the mixing bowl mix up almond flour, butter, and 1 tablespoon of Erythritol. Knead the dough.

2.   Transfer the dough in the cheesecake mold and flatten it to get the pie crust shape. Place it in the freezer for 10 minutes.

3.   Meanwhile, put the cream cheese, egg, coconut milk, pumpkin pie spices, and remaining Erythritol in the mixing bowl. Mix the mixture until smooth with the help of the hand mixer.

4.   Pour the cream cheese mixture over the frozen pie crust, flatten it well.

5.   Pour water and insert the steamer rack in the instant pot and put the cheesecake on it.

6.   Close and seal the lid.

7.   Cook it on manual (high pressure) for 30 minutes. Make a quick pressure release.

Nutritional info per serve: calories 156, fat 15.2, fiber 0.5, carbs 7.6, protein 3.6

Daikon Cake

Prep time: 10 minutes | **Cook time:** 45 minutes | **Yield:** 12 servings

Ingredients

5 eggs, beaten

½ cup heavy cream

1 cup almond flour

1 daikon, diced

1 teaspoon ground cinnamon

2 tablespoon Erythritol

1 tablespoon butter, melted

1 cup water, for cooking

Method

1.   In the mixing bowl, mix up eggs, heavy cream, almond flour, ground cinnamon, and Erythritol.

2.   When the mixture is smooth, add daikon and stir it carefully with the help of the spatula.

3.   Pour the mixture in the cake pan.

4.   Then pour water and insert the steamer rack in the instant pot.

5.   Place the cake in the instant pot.

6.   Close and seal the lid.

7.   Cook the cake in manual mode (high pressure) for 45 minutes. Make a quick pressure release.

Nutritional info per serve: calories 67, fat 5.8, fiber 0.4, carbs 3.6, protein 3

Almond Pie

Prep time: 15 minutes | **Cook time:** 41 minutes | **Yield:** 8 servings

Ingredients

1 cup almond flour

½ cup of coconut milk

1 teaspoon vanilla extract

2 tablespoons butter, softened

1 tablespoon Truvia

¼ cup coconut, shredded

1 cup water, for cooking

Method

1.   In the mixing bowl, mix up almond flour, coconut milk, vanilla extract, butter, Truvia, and shredded coconut.

2.   When the mixture is smooth, transfer it in the baking pan and flatten.

3.   Pour water and insert the steamer rack in the instant pot.

4.   Put the baking pan with cake on the rack. Close and seal the lid.

5.   Cook the dessert on manual mode (high pressure) for 41 minutes. Allow the natural pressure release for 10 minutes.

Nutritional info per serve: calories 90, fat 9.1, fiber 0.9, carbs 2.6, protein 1.2

Coconut Cupcakes

Prep time: 15 minutes | **Cook time:** 10 minutes | **Yield:** 6 servings

Ingredients

4 eggs, beaten

4 tablespoons coconut milk

4 tablespoons coconut flour

½ teaspoon vanilla extract

2 tablespoons Erythritol

1 teaspoon baking powder

1 cup water, for cooking

Method

1.   In the mixing bowl, mix up eggs, coconut milk, coconut flour, vanilla extract, Erythritol, and baking powder.

2.   Then pour the batter in the cupcake molds.

3.   Pour water and insert the steamer rack in the instant pot.

4.   Place the cupcakes on the rack. Close and seal the lid.

5.   Cook the cupcakes for 10 minutes on manual mode (high pressure).

6.   Then allow the natural pressure release for 5 minutes.

Nutritional info per serve: calories 86, fat 5.8, fiber 2.2, carbs 9.2, protein 4.6

Anise Hot Chocolate

Prep time: 10 minutes | **Cook time:** 2 minutes | **Yield:** 3 servings

Ingredients

1 tablespoon cocoa powder

1 tablespoon Erythritol

¼ cup heavy cream

½ cup of coconut milk

½ teaspoon ground anise

Method

1.   Put all ingredients in the instant pot bowl. Stir them well until you get a smooth liquid.

2.   Close and seal the lid.

3.   Cook the hot chocolate on manual (high pressure) for 2 minutes. Then allow the natural pressure release for 5 minutes.

Nutritional info per serve: calories 131, fat 13.5, fiber 1.4, carbs 8.5, protein 1.5

Chocolate Mousse

Prep time: 10 minutes | **Cook time:** 4 minutes | **Yield:** 1 serving

Ingredients

1 egg yolk

1 teaspoon Erythritol

1 teaspoon of cocoa powder

2 tablespoons coconut milk

1 tablespoon cream cheese

1 cup water, for cooking

Method

1.   Pour water and insert the steamer rack in the instant pot.

2.   Then whisk the egg yolk with Erythritol.

3.   When the mixture turns into lemon color, add coconut milk, cream cheese, and cocoa powder. Whisk the mixture until smooth.

4.   Then pour it in the glass jar and place it on the steamer rack.

5.   Close and seal the lid.

6.   Cook the dessert on manual (high pressure) for 4 minutes. Make a quick pressure release.

Nutritional info per serve: calories 162, fat 15.4, fiber 1.2, carbs 3.5, protein 4.5

Lime Muffins

Prep time: 10 minutes | **Cook time:** 15 minutes | **Yield:** 6 servings

Ingredients

1 teaspoon lime zest

1 tablespoon lemon juice

1 teaspoon baking powder

1 cup almond flour

2 eggs, beaten

1 tablespoon swerve

¼ cup heavy cream

1 cup water, for cooking

Method

1.   In the mixing bowl, mix up lemon juice, baking powder, almond flour, eggs, swerve, and heavy cream.

2.   When the muffin batter is smooth, add lime zest and mix it up.

3.   Fill the muffin molds with batter.

4.   Then pour water and insert the rack in the instant pot.

5.   Place the muffins on the rack. Close and seal the lid.

6.   Cook the muffins on manual (high pressure) for 15 minutes.

7.   Then allow the natural pressure release.

Nutritional info per serve: calories 153, fat 12.2, fiber 2.1, carbs 5.1, protein 6

Blueberry Muffins

Prep time: 15 minutes | **Cook time:** 14 minutes
| **Yield: 3** servings

Ingredients

¼ cup blueberries

¼ teaspoon baking powder

1 teaspoon apple cider vinegar

4 teaspoons butter, melted

2 eggs, beaten

1 cup coconut flour

2 tablespoons Erythritol

1 cup water, for cooking

Method

1.   In the mixing bowl, mix up baking powder, apple cider vinegar, butter, eggs, coconut flour, and Erythritol.

2.   When the batter is smooth, add blueberries. Stir well.

3.   Put the muffin batter in the muffin molds.

4.   After this, pour water and insert the steamer rack in the instant pot.

5.   Then place the muffins on the rack. Close and seal the lid.

6.   Cook the muffins on manual mode (high pressure) for 14 minutes.

7.   When the time is finished, allow the natural pressure release for 6 minutes.

Nutritional info per serve: calories 95, fat 4.5, fiber 6.1, carbs 14.6, protein 3.4

Low Carb Brownie

Prep time: 15 minutes | **Cook time:** 15 minutes
| **Yield:** 8 servings

Ingredients

1 cup coconut flour

1 tablespoon cocoa powder

1 tablespoon coconut oil

1 teaspoon vanilla extract

1 teaspoon baking powder

1 teaspoon apple cider vinegar

1/3 cup butter, melted

1 tablespoon Erythritol

1 cup water, for cooking

Method

1.   In the mixing bowl, mix up Erythritol, melted butter, apple cider vinegar, baking powder, vanilla extract, coconut oil, cocoa powder, and coconut flour.

2.   Whisk the mixture until smooth and pour it in the baking pan. Flatten the surface of the batter.

3.   Pour water and insert the steamer rack in the instant pot.

4.   Put the pan with brownie batter on the rack. Close and seal the lid.

5.   Cook the brownie on manual mode (high pressure) for 15 minutes.

6.   Then allow the natural pressure release for 5 minutes.

7.   Cut the cooked brownies into the bars.

Nutritional info per serve: calories 146, fat 11, fiber 6.2, carbs 12.6, protein 2.2

Pecan Pie

Prep time: 20 minutes | **Cook time:** 25 minutes | **Yield:** 4 servings

Ingredients

2 tablespoons coconut oil

4 tablespoons almond flour

4 pecans, chopped

1 tablespoon Erythritol

2 tablespoons butter

1 tablespoon coconut flour

1 cup water, for cooking

Method

1.   Make the pie crust: mix up coconut oil and almond flour in the bowl.

2.   Then knead the dough and put it in the baking pan. Flatten the dough in the shape of the pie crust.

3.   Then melt Erythritol, butter, and coconut flour.

4.   When the mixture is liquid, add chopped pecans.

5.   Pour water in the instant pot and insert the steamer rack.

6.   Pour the butter-pecan mixture over the pie crust, flatten it and transfer on the steamer rack.

7.   Cook the pecan pie on manual mode (high pressure) for 25 minutes.

8.   Allow the natural pressure release for 10 minutes and cool the cooked pie well.

Nutritional info per serve: calories 257, fat 26.1, fiber 3, carbs 8.5, protein 3.3

Vanilla Flan

Prep time: 10 minutes | **Cook time:** 8 minutes | **Yield:** 4 servings

Ingredients

4 egg whites

4 egg yolks

½ cup Erythritol

7 oz heavy cream, whipped

3 tablespoons water

1 tablespoon butter

½ teaspoon vanilla extract

1 cup water, for cooking

Method

1.   In the saucepan, heat up Erythritol and butter. When the mixture is smooth, leave it in a warm place.

2.   Meanwhile, mix up water, heavy cream, egg whites, and egg yolks. Whisk the mixture.

3.   Pour the Erythritol mixture in the flan ramekins and then add heavy cream mixture over the sweet mixture.

4.   Pour water and insert the steamer rack in the instant pot.

5.   Place the ramekins with flan on the rack. Close and seal the lid.

6.   Cook the dessert on manual (high pressure) for 10 minutes. Then allow the natural pressure release for 10 minutes.

7.   Cool the cooked flan for 25 minutes.

Nutritional info per serve: calories 269, fat 25.8, fiber 0, carbs 2.3, protein 7.4

Vanilla Pie

Prep time: 20 minutes | **Cook time:** 35 minutes | **Yield:** 12 servings

Ingredients

1 cup heavy cream

3 eggs, beaten

1 teaspoon vanilla extract

¼ cup Erythritol

1 cup coconut flour

1 tablespoon butter, melted

1 cup water, for cooking

Method

1.   In the mixing bowl, mix up coconut flour, Erythritol, vanilla extract, eggs, and heavy cream.

2.   Grease the baking pan with melted butter.

3.   Pour the coconut mixture in the baking pan.

4.   Pour water and insert the steamer rack in the instant pot.

5.   Place the pie on the rack. Close and seal the lid.

6.   Cook the pie on manual mode (high pressure) for 35 minutes.

7.   Allow the natural pressure release for 10 minutes.

Nutritional info per serve: calories 100, fat 6.8, fiber 4, carbs 12.1, protein 2.9

Custard

Prep time: 10 minutes | **Cook time:** 7 minutes | **Yield:** 4 servings

Ingredients

6 eggs, beaten

1 cup heavy cream

1 teaspoon vanilla extract

¼ teaspoon ground nutmeg

2 tablespoons Erythritol

1 tablespoon coconut flour

1 cup water, for cooking

Method

1.   Whisk the eggs and Erythritol until smooth.

2.   Then add heavy cream, vanilla extract, ground nutmeg, and coconut flour.

3.   Whisk the mixture well again.

4.   Then pour it in the custard ramekins and cover with foil.

5.   Pour water and insert the steamer rack in the instant pot.

6.   Place the ramekins with custard on the rack. Close and seal the lid.

7.   Cook the meal on manual (high pressure) for 7 minutes. Make a quick pressure release.

Nutritional info per serve: calories 209, fat 17.9, fiber 0.8, carbs 10.3, protein 9.2

Crème Brule

Prep time: 25 minutes | **Cook time:** 10 minutes | **Yield:** 2 servings

Ingredients

1 cup heavy cream

5 egg yolks

2 tablespoons swerve

1 cup water, for cooking

Method

1.   Whisk the egg yolks and swerve together.

2.   Then add heavy cream and stir the mixture carefully.

3.   Pour the mixture in ramekins and place them on the steamer rack.

4.   Pour water in the instant pot. Add steamer rack with ramekins.

5.   Close and seal the lid.

6.   Cook crème Brule for 10 minutes – High pressure. Allow the natural pressure release for 15 minutes.

Nutritional info per serve: calories 347, fat 33.5, fiber 0, carbs 5.2, protein 8

Lava Cake

Prep time: 15 minutes | **Cook time:** 18 minutes | **Yield:** 4 servings

Ingredients

1 teaspoon baking powder

1 tablespoon cocoa powder

1 cup coconut cream

1/3 cup coconut flour

1 tablespoon almond flour

2 teaspoons Erythritol

1 tablespoon butter, melted

1 cup water, for cooking

Method

1.   Whisk together baking powder, cocoa powder, coconut cream, coconut flour, almond flour, Erythritol, and butter.

2.   Then pour the chocolate mixture in the baking cups.

3.   Pour water in the instant pot. Insert the steamer rack.

4.   Place the cups with cake mixture on the rack. Close and seal the lid.

5.   Cook the lava cakes on manual (high pressure) for 4 minutes. Allow the natural pressure release for 5 minutes.

Nutritional info per serve: calories 218, fat 19.2, fiber 5.9, carbs 14.2, protein 3.4

Cinnamon Roll

Prep time: 15 minutes | **Cook time:** 20 minutes | **Yield:** 4 servings

Ingredients

1 tablespoon ground cinnamon

1 tablespoon butter, softened

2 tablespoons coconut oil

1 tablespoon Erythritol

½ cup almond flour

½ teaspoon baking powder

1 cup water, for cooking

Method

1.   In the mixing bowl, mix up coconut oil, almond flour, and baking powder. Knead the dough.

2.   Then roll it up and grease with butter.

3.   Then sprinkle the dough with Erythritol and ground cinnamon.

4.   Roll the dough into a log and cut on buns.

5.   Pour water in the instant pot and insert the steamer rack.

6.   Put the cinnamon rolls (buns) in the baking pan and transfer it on the rack.

7.   Close and seal the lid.

8.   Cook the dessert on manual mode (high pressure) for 20 minutes. Make a quick pressure release.

Nutritional info per serve: calories 173, fat 16.4, fiber 2.4, carbs 4.7, protein 3.1

Peanut Bars

Prep time: 25 minutes | **Cook time:** 12 minutes | **Yield:** 4 servings

Ingredients

2 tablespoons coconut oil

2 oz peanuts, chopped

2 tablespoons Swerve

½ teaspoon baking powder

4 tablespoons coconut flour

1 tablespoon butter, softened

1 teaspoon of cocoa powder

1 cup water, for cooking

Method

1.   Make the pie crust: knead the dough from butter, coconut flour, and baking powder.

2.   Then put the dough in the pie mold and flatten it.

3.   Pour water and insert the rack in the instant pot.

4.   Put the pie crust in the instant pot. Close and seal the lid.

5.   Cook it on manual mode (high pressure) for 12 minutes. Make a quick pressure release.

6.   Meanwhile, mix up peanuts, coconut oil, Swerve, and cocoa powder. Melt the mixture.

7.   When the pie crust is cooked, pour the peanut mixture over it and cool it.

Nutritional info per serve: calories 199, fat 17.5, fiber 4.3, carbs 8.8, protein 4.8

Cocoa Cookie

Prep time: 15 minutes | **Cook time:** 25 minutes | **Yield:** 4 servings

Ingredients

½ cup coconut flour

3 tablespoons cream cheese

1 teaspoon of cocoa powder

1 tablespoon Erythritol

¼ teaspoon baking powder

1 teaspoon apple cider vinegar

1 tablespoon butter

1 cup water, for cooking

Method

1.   Make the dough: mix up coconut flour, cream cheese, cocoa powder, Erythritol, baking powder, apple cider vinegar, and butter. Knead the dough,

2.   Then transfer the dough in the baking pan and flatten it in the shape of a cookie.

3.   Pour water and insert the steamer rack in the instant pot.

4.   Put the pan with a cookie in the instant pot. Close and seal the lid.

5.   Cook the cookie on manual (high pressure) for 25 minutes. Make a quick pressure release. Cool the cookie well.

Nutritional info per serve: calories 113, fat 7.1, fiber 6.1, carbs 14.4, protein 2.7

Red Velvet Muffins

Prep time: 10 minutes | **Cook time:** 15 minutes | **Yield:** 2 servings

Ingredients

¼ teaspoon red food coloring

2 teaspoons butter

¼ teaspoon baking powder

1 teaspoon apple cider vinegar

4 tablespoons coconut flour

1 teaspoon vanilla extract

3 tablespoons heavy cream

1 cup water, for cooking

Method

1. In the mixing bowl, mix up red food coloring, butter, baking powder, apple cider vinegar, coconut flour, vanilla extract, and heavy cream.

2. Stir the mixture until it is smooth.

3. After this, pour the mixture in the muffin molds.

4. Pour water and insert the steamer rack in the instant pot.

5. Place the muffin molds on the rack. Close and seal the lid.

6. Cook the muffins on manual (high pressure) for 15 minutes. Make a quick pressure release.

Nutritional info per serve: calories 179, fat 13.6, fiber 6, carbs 11.2, protein 2.5

Pecan Pralines

Prep time: 15 minutes | **Cook time:** 7 minutes | **Yield:** 4 servings

Ingredients

4 pecans

4 teaspoons coconut oil

1 teaspoon of cocoa powder

1 teaspoon Erythritol

Method

1. Heat up the instant pot on saute mode.

2. Then add coconut oil and cocoa powder. Saute the mixture until it is smooth and homogenous.

3. Meanwhile, line the tray with baking paper.

4. Put the pecans on the baking paper.

5. Pour the hot coconut oil mixture over the pecans. Refrigerate the pralines for 10-15 minutes.

Nutritional info per serve: calories 138, fat 14.6, fiber 1.6, carbs 3.5, protein 1.6

Vanilla Hot Drink

Prep time: 2 minutes | **Cook time:** 7 minutes | **Yield:** 2 servings

Ingredients

1 cup almond milk

1 teaspoon butter

1 teaspoon vanilla extract

1 teaspoon erythritol

1 tablespoon cocoa powder

Method

1. Transfer all the ingredients into the instant pot bowl.

2. Set the "Saute" and start to cook the hot chocolate.

3. Saute the hot chocolate until it starts to boil. (around 10 minutes).

Nutritional info per serve: calories 29, fat 3.8, fiber 0.8, carbs 4.3, protein 1

RECIPE INDEX

"Ramen" Soup **57**

A

Alaskan Crab Legs 100

Almond Pie 115

Anise Hot Chocolate 115

Apple Cider Vinegar Ham 77

Apple Cider Vinegar Mussels 98

Aromatic Pork Belly 74

Asian Ribs 72

B

Bacon and Cheese Bites 27

Bacon Avocado Bomb 30

Bacon Casserole 33

Bacon Deviled Eggs 36

Bacon Peppers 40

Bang Bang Shrimps 98

Basil Pork Loin 79

BBQ Baby Back Ribs 73

Beef Burgundy 61

Beef Gyros Stuffing 62

Beef Pot Roast 59

Beef Pot Round Steak 60

Beef Stew 52

Beef Tagine 58

Beef Vindaloo 65

Bell Peppers with Omelet 30

Blackened Salmon 99

BLT Dip 37

Blueberry Muffins 117

Boiled Crawfish 101

Breakfast Casserole 25

Breakfast Sandwich 28

Breakfast Taco Skillet 31

Broccoli Cheese Soup 49

Broccoli Skewers 47

Butter Beef 62

Butter Chicken 86

Butter Clams 104

C

Cabbage Soup 51

Cajun Cod 100

Carnitas Pulled Pork 71

Cauliflower Fritters 43

Cauliflower Gnocchi 112

Cauliflower Queso 35

Cauliflower Soup 51

Cauliflower Tikka Masala 108

Cheese Chicken Kofte 94

Cheese Jalapenos 39

Cheese Roll-Ups 31

Cheese Stuffed Shishito Peppers 42

Cheeseburger Soup 51

Cheesy Cream Soup 54

Chicken Alfredo 87

Chicken Celery Sticks 41

Chicken Curry with Cilantro 91

Chicken Fingers 96

Chicken in Gravy 86

Chicken Jalapenos Roll 91

Chicken Lombardy 95

Chicken Masala 90

Chicken Nuggets 92

Chicken Paprikash 52

Chicken Pasta 89

Chicken Soup 49

Chicken with Pizza Stuffing 96

Chicken&Chinese Cabbage Salad 43

Chili Haddock 103
Chipotle Stew 55
Chives Mushrooms 112
Chocolate Mousse 116
Chorizo Soup 57
Cilantro Pork Shoulder 76
Cinnamon Roll 120
Cioppino Stew 98
Clam Chowder 103
Classic Meatballs 36
Cocoa Cookie 121
Coconut Cupcakes 115
Coconut Shrimps 39
Cod with Olives 107
Cordon Bleu 88
Crack Chicken 84
Crème Brule 119
Curry Stew with Chicken 52
Custard 119

D
Daikon Cake 114
Dijon Turkey Meatballs 93

E
Egg Cups 26
Egg Cups on the Run 34
Eggplant Bites 40
Eggs Benedict 25

F
Fabulous Cilantro Meatballs 79
Fajita Strips 92
Fat Bombs 41
Faux-Tatoes 46
Feta Psiti 45
Fiesta Chicken 89
Fish Curry 104

Frittata with Greens 26

G
Garlic Chicken with Lemon 84
Garlic Shirataki Noodles 47
Giant Vanilla Pancake 29
Goulash 60
Greek Burger 93
Greek Style Leg of Lamb 62
Ground Pork Pizza Crust 81
Ground Pork Stroganoff 80
Gumbo 49

H
Harissa Lamb Shoulder 66
Herbed Pork Tenderloin 76
Herbed Radish 111
Herbed Whole Chicken 88
Hibachi Steak 61

I
Icelandic Lamb 66
Italian Style Lamb Stew 53
Italian Style Salmon 103

J
Jicama Mash 111
Juicy Chicken Breast 85

K
Kale and Eggs Bake 32
Kale Stir Fry 109
Keto Chili 55
Kofta Curry 67
Koobideh 67

L
Lamb Bhuna 64
Lamb Burger 68
Lamb Curry 63

Lamb Kleftiko 64
Lamb Masala 65
Lamb Roast 64
Lamb Shank with Spices 62
Lamb Soup 56
Lava Cake 120
Lemon Mushrooms 45
Lemon Salmon 101
Lime Mahi Mahi 105
Lime Muffins 116
Louisiana Gumbo 100
Low Carb Brownie 117

M
Margherita Egg Cups 34
Mashed Turnips 113
Meat and Cauliflower Bake 32
Meat Cups 29
Meatloaf with Eggs 78
Minestrone Soup 56
Mississippi Pork 73
Mongolian Beef 59
Morning Burritos 28
Mozzarella Stuffed Meatballs 82
Mustard Chicken Breast 86

N
Noatmeal 27

O
Okra and Beef Stew 54

P
Pancetta Wings 97
Paprika Chicken Wings 88
Paprika Ribs 75
Parm Zucchini Noodles 108
Parmesan Balls with Greens 42
Parmesan Chicken Fillets 87

Peanut Bars 121
Pecan Pie 118
Pecan Pralines 122
Peppercorn Pork 76
Peppered Lamb Ribs 70
Persian Lamb 63
Pesto Flounder 106
Pesto Rack of Lamb 67
Philadelphia Stuffed Chicken Breast 96
Pizza Soup 55
Poblano Chicken Strips 95
Pork Chops Al Pastor 82
Pork Chops with Blue Cheese 71
Pork Milanese 80
Pork Ragu 77
Pork Stew 53
Pork Tenders 74
Provolone Stuffed Chicken 97
Pulled Chicken 90
Pulled Pork Hash with Eggs 32
Pulpo Gallego 102
Pumpkin Pie Spices Cheesecake 114

R
Ranch Pork Chops 75
Red Cauliflower Rice 44
Red Feta Soup 57
Red Velvet Muffins 121
Reuben Pickles 41
Roasted Tomatillos 43
Rogan Josh 65
Romano Pork Chops 81
Rosemary Catfish Steak 105
Rosemary Chicken Wings 35

S
Salmon Cakes 105

Salmon Caprese 106
Sausage Balls 37
Sausage Dip 38
Scallion Dip 40
Seafood Stew 54
Seafood Zoodle Alfredo 107
Sesame Broccoli Sprouts 46
Sesame Chicken 90
Shami Kabob 68
Shrimp Curry with Coconut Milk 99
Shrimp Sandwich 48
Shrimp Skewers 104
Smoked Sausages Cabbage 83
Smoky Chicken Breast 94
Smothered Pork Chops 78
Spiced Broccoli 111
Spiced Cauliflower Head 108
Spicy Cod 102
Spinach Dip 37
Spinach Tuna Cakes 101
Starbucks Eggs 25
Steak Bites 60
Steamed Fennel Bulb 47
Steamed Kohlrabi 46
Steamed Rostelle 69
Steamed Savoy Cabbage 45
Steamed Spinach with Garlic 44
Stew Cubes 80
Stuffed Hard-Boiled Eggs 30
Stuffed Mushrooms 38
Stuffed Pork Rolls 74
Sub Salad 83
Swedish Meatballs 33
Sweet Pork Tenderloin 71

Sweet Smokies 35

T
Taco Bites 38
Taco Casserole 82
Taco Soup 50
Tempeh Satay 109
Tender Chicken Thighs 91
Tender Turkey Tetrazzini 94
Teriyaki Eggplants 109
Thyme Beef Brisket 59
Thyme Cabbage 110
Thyme Chicken Gizzards 93
Thyme Lobster Tails 99
Thyme Pork Meatballs 72
Tofu Quiche 110
Turmeric Pork Strips 78
Tuscan Chicken 84
Tuscan Soup 50

V
Vanilla Flan 118
Vanilla Hot Drink 122
Vanilla Pie 119
Veal Meatloaf 69
Vietnamese Pork 73

W
White Cabbage Hash Browns 28
White Chicken Chili 85
Wrapped Pork Cubes 75

Z
Zucchini Cheese Tots 44
Zucchini Fritters 112